Best
TEA SHOP WALKS
in
MID WALES

Dorothy Hamilton

Published by Sigma Leisure – an imprint of
Sigma Press, 5 Alton Road, Wilmslow, Cheshire SK9 5DY, England.

British Library Cataloguing in Publication Data
A CIP record for this book is available from the British Library.

ISBN: 1-85058-796-5

Cover photograph: the lake at Tal-y-Llyn *(Graham Beech)*

Maps: Jeremy Semmens, based on sketches derived from the author's own observations

Photographs: the author

Typesetting and Design by: Sigma Press, Wilmslow, Cheshire.

Printed by: Ashford Colour Press Ltd

Contents

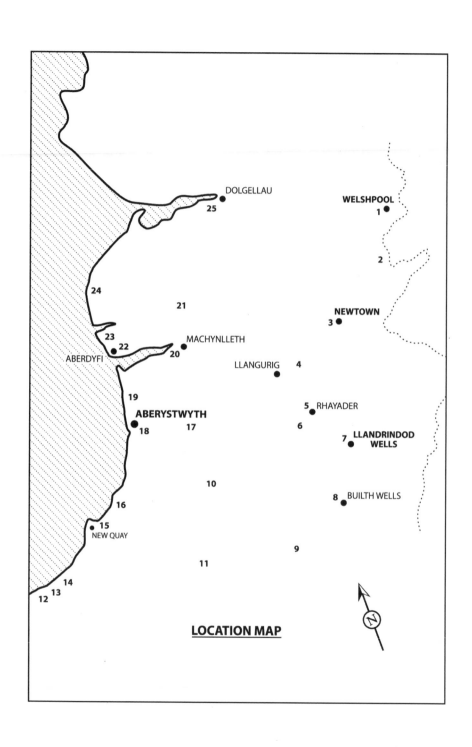

DOLGELLAU
25

WELSHPOOL
1

2

24

21

NEWTOWN
3

23
22

MACHYNLLETH
20

ABERDYFI

LLANGURIG 4

19

5 RHAYADER

ABERYSTWYTH

18 17 6

7 LLANDRINDOD
WELLS

10

8 BUILTH WELLS

16

15
NEW QUAY

9

11

14
12 13

LOCATION MAP

N

Introduction

Mid Wales comprises a vast area with scenery ranging from mountains, moorland and green valleys to woodlands and coastal cliffs. This beautiful, tranquil region has much to offer the walker.

Near the English border, historic towns stand close to Offa's great embankment. Here, Marcher lords built their castles and those at Welshpool and Montgomery are visited on walks. If you follow the River Severn west from Welshpool, you will pass through Newtown and Llanidloes. The latter is the first town on this river which has its headwaters on Plynlimon, the highest mountain in this part of Wales. Plynlimon is also the source of the delightful River Wye which flows through Rhayader and Builth Wells, both starting points of walks.

Lakes in the form of reservoirs are major landmarks in Mid Wales and those in the Elan Valley are the most famous of all. Watch the skies for the red kite on the walk from the Visitor Centre and on other walks, especially around Tregaron. Near this small town is the largest bog in Wales.

The drinking of mineral waters became the fashion in the 18th century and, on their discovery in Mid Wales, a string of spa towns was established. At Llandrindod Wells you can still drink waters from the chalybeate spring (see page 42).

Much of the Ceredigion coastline is designated Heritage Coast whilst Cardigan Bay is home to over one hundred bottle-nosed dolphins as well as porpoises and grey seals. Picturesque villages and coastal resorts are the starting points for spectacular cliff walks. More outstanding scenery can be enjoyed on walks north of the Dyfi estuary on the coast and in the foothills of southern Snowdonia.

The first visitors to Wales arrived in the Palaeolithic era when Britain was, at one stage, part of the European land mass. Several caves in north and south Wales have yielded evidence of Stone Age man.

Celtic people from Central Europe arrived about 600BC, the start of the Iron age. Although they lived in farmsteads and centred their lives around agriculture, they built defensive forts on hilltops and coastal promontories. Several families lived in an enclosure surrounded by ditches and banks.

Hill forts feature on several walks including those from Montgomery, Lampeter and Aberystwyth. Coastal promontory forts were protected by cliffs and only the neck of the headland needed banks and ditches. Eventually, these Celtic people formed tribes and when the Romans arrived there were five main tribes in Wales: the Silures in the south-east, the Demetae in the south-west, the Ordovices in the north-west and the Cornovii and Deceangli in the north and east. The Romans built a system of roads, marching camps and forts but the campaign in Wales was not completed until AD77. Castell Collen Roman fort near Llandrindod Wells was built in several phases and held a garrison of 400 to 1000 men.

The period from the Roman withdrawal until the coming of the Normans is sometimes referred to as the Dark Ages. In Wales, during these seven centuries, there was a revival of Celtic culture. The Romans had introduced Christianity to Britain and missionaries from Brittany and Ireland founded churches and monasteries. No buildings have survived from this period but some early Christian stones remain. A 5th- to 7th-century inscribed stone can be seen in the Church of St Cadfan on the walk starting at Tywyn.

Wales gradually formed into a number of small kingdoms under separate rulers. In the late 8th century, King Offa of Mercia built his great earthwork as a defence against the Welsh. During the following century Rhodri Mawr (the Great) united most of Wales by marrying the heiress of Ceredigion. His grandson Hywel Dda (the Good) ruled all the kingdoms of Wales except those in the south-east. He issued his own coinage but when he died Wales reverted again into separate kingdoms.

After their conquest of England in AD1066, the Normans slowly penetrated Wales by building a series of motte and bailey castles. Visible remains are Hen Domen near Montgomery, built by the Earl of Shrewsbury about 1080, and Builth Castle erected by William de Braose. Strong Welsh leaders were successful in halting the Normans' progress, especially Lord Rhys of Deheubarth who built Rhayader Castle. The Normans introduced a new system of agriculture and reorganised the church. Monasteries were established and one of the most notable in Mid Wales was Strata Florida, which became renowned as a centre of Welsh culture and learning. Founded as a Cistercian abbey in 1164 by the Norman Robert fitz Stephen, it was moved to the present site by Lord Rhys when he gained power in Ceredigion. According to tradition, the great medieval poet Dafydd ap Gwilym was buried in the abbey.

At the beginning of the 13th century, Llywelyn ap Iorwerth became the most powerful of the medieval princes. By the time of his death in 1240, he ruled most of Wales. His grandson Llywelyn ap Gruffudd was acknowledged Prince of Wales by Henry III. When Edward I succeeded to the throne in 1272, Llywelyn refused to do homage. The king declared war and, after a long campaign, Llywelyn was killed in December 1282 near Builth Wells. His death brought an end to Welsh independence and it was now the king's eldest son who received the title Prince of Wales. Edward consolidated his victory by building many stone castles, including one at Aberystwyth. He divided Llywelyn's principality into English-type shires. In Mid Wales this created Merionethshire and Cardiganshire whilst east and much of south Wales remained in the hands of the Marcher Lords.

In September 1400, Owain Glyndwr, a descendant of the royal houses of Powys and Deheubarth, led an uprising against the English which was to last ten years. He captured a number of castles including those of Aberystwyth and Harlech. Machynlleth was his chosen capital of Wales and it is said he was crowned there in the presence of envoys from France, Castile and Scotland. He had plans for two universities in Wales, one in the north and one in the south. Gradually, the rebellion petered out, Aberystwyth Castle was lost in 1408, and his family were taken prisoner at Harlech. It is not known how Owain ended his days.

After the Acts of Union of England and Wales, the Marcher lordships were abolished and the new shires of Radnor and Montgomery were created in Mid Wales. English law replaced Welsh law and the language of the courts was English. Welsh gentry became justices of the peace. However, this had the effect of anglicising the ruling classes and separated them from the Welsh speaking population.

Until the coming of the railways, drovers played a vital part in rural Wales. In the mid 18th century, 30,000 Welsh cattle were driven to English markets every year. Drovers even established local banks such as the Bank of the Black Sheep in Aberystwyth whilst, along some drovers' routes, settlements grew at points where cattle were gathered and shod for their journey. Some of the inns where drovers stayed can be seen today.

Sheep farmers and their families earned extra income by making cloth at home. Carding, spinning and weaving were carried out in isolated cottages and farmhouses before the cloth was finished in a water-driven fulling mill and exported to England. When mechanical carding and spinning was invented, many small factories were set up beside rivers. Llanidloes and Newtown became important centres.

Fishing was an important supplementary income for those who lived near the sea. In the mid 18th century, fishermen in Cardigan Bay often caught huge shoals of herring and mackerel. The fish were preserved by being salted or smoked, sometimes both, before being exported to markets throughout Britain or farther afield. Aberporth and Aberystwyth became two of the principal herring ports in Wales. Fish such as salmon and grey mullet were caught in traps at Aberporth. Before the improvement of roads and the coming of the railways, goods were transported by sea to and from the coastal settlements. Sloops were built locally as needed whilst New Quay and Aberaeron established shipbuilding yards.

On the coming of the railways, Victorians popularised the coastal resorts whilst health seekers took the scenic Heart of Wales Line to the fashionable spas. Present day visitors to Mid Wales come to explore the dramatic coastline and rich landscape with its historical villages and towns.

The Tea Shops

By ending your walk at a tea room, you experience the best combination of a day out in Wales – an easy or moderate walk through beautiful scenery followed by an appetising light meal. All the tea shops welcome walkers but please be considerate and remove wet waterproofs and clean or remove muddy boots.

As well as cream teas, many of the tea shops offer Welsh specialities such as bara brith, a yeast fruit bread. Welsh cakes are a kind of griddle cake that contains dried fruit. Most tea rooms provide home cooking, especially home-made cakes.

The establishments chosen are varied and include old church rooms, schoolrooms, a castle, a former cobbler's shop and the Old Pump Room at Llandrindod Wells spa. Many are in very old buildings. Some tea rooms are attached to Visitor Centres where you can obtain information about the local area.

The majority of the tea shops are open all year. If walking early or late in the year, it is advisable to check opening times. Most of the tea rooms would appreciate advance notice of a large walking group.

The Walks

Apart from the walk between Borth and Aberystwyth, all the walks in this guide are circular. They explore a wide variety of countryside from woodlands, moorland and hillsides to coastal cliffs. Although routes range from 2½ to 9½ miles, most are between 3½ and 6 miles. Almost all the walks are suitable for families, but children must be closely supervised, especially on cliffs and near water. In windy weather avoid cliff paths. Some walks are fairly level but most require a little climbing. Allow plenty of time to complete the walks, especially in the winter. High mountain routes are not included.

Boots are not essential for all the routes but they are recommended for their ankle support and protection on rough or muddy paths. Warm clothing, including head covering and gloves, are essential in the winter. Waterproofs should be carried when there is a possibility of rain. On longer walks, you may like to carry light refreshments and drinks for a picnic, especially if there are children in the group.

Each walk includes detailed directions and a sketch map. You may like to carry the relevant Ordnance Survey map as well – it would help you to identify the features around you, and places not mentioned in the text. The maps referred to are Nos. 187, 188, 198, 199, 200, 213, 214, 215 and 216 in the Explorer (1:25 000) series. A few walks are on the No. 23 Outdoor Leisure Map (the latest of these maps are now in the Explorer series).

Public Transport

Almost all the walks are accessible by public transport. Details are given for each walk. Free timetables are available at Tourist Information Centres.

Useful Phone Numbers

Traveline Cymru: 0870 608 2 608

Arriva Cymru: 01654 702239

Aberaeron Tourist Information Centre: 01545 570602

Aberdyfi Tourist Information Centre: 01654 767321

Aberystwyth Tourist Information Centre: 01970 612125

Borth Tourist Information Centre: 01970 612125

Builth Wells Tourist Information Centre: 01982 553307

Cardigan Tourist Information Centre: 01239 613230

Corris Tourist Information Centre: 01654 761244

Dolgellau Tourist Information Centre: 01341 422888

Elan Valley Tourist Information Centre: 01597 810898

Llanidloes Tourist Information Centre: 01686 412605

Llandrindod Wells Tourist Information Centre: 01597 822600

Llanwrtyd Wells Tourist Information Centre: 01591 610666

Machynlleth Tourist Information Centre: 01654 702401

New Quay Tourist Information Centre: 01545 560865

Newtown Tourist Information Centre: 01686 625580

Rhayader Tourist Information Centre: 01597 810591

Tywyn Tourist Information Centre: 01654 710070

Welshpool Tourist Information Centre: 01938 552043

Welsh Place Names

Place names in Wales can sometimes cause problems. Learning these pronunciations will help:

A	ah
C	k (hard)
Ch	as in 'loch'
Dd	'th' as in 'the'
E	eh
F	v
Ff	f
G	as in 'go'
I	ee
Ll	say 'l', hold the tongue in position and blow gently
O	oh
Th	as in 'through'
W	usually as in oo (cwm sounds like coom)
Y	as e in 'the'

The following translations will help in understanding Welsh place names. Some refer to geographical features or have historical connections:

Abaty	abbey
Aber	estuary, river mouth
Afon	river
Bach/fach	small
Brith	speckled
Bryn	hill
Bwa	arch
Bwlch	pass
Bychan	little
Cae	field
Caer	fort
Canol	middle/centre
Capel	chapel
Carreg	rock
Castell	castle
Cau	hollow
Cefn	ridge
Ceunant	ravine
Clogwyn	cliff
Coch	red
Coed	woodland
Cors/gors	bog, marsh
Craig	crag
Croes	cross
Cwm	valley
Cwrt	court
Dinas	fort
Dol/ddol	meadow
Drws	door
Du/ddu	black
Dwr	water
Dyffryn	valley
Eglwys	church

Esgair	ridge, mountain shoulder
Ffordd	road
Ffridd	mountain pasture
Ffynnon	well, spring
Gallt/allt	hillside, slope
Garth	hill, enclosure
Glan	riverbank
Glas	blue, green
Gorsaf	station
Gwastad	level ground
Gwaun/waun	moor
Gwyn	white
Hafod/hafoty	summer dwelling
Hen	old
Hendre	winter dwelling
Heol	street
Isaf	lower
Llan	church
Llethr	slope
Llety	lodging, inn
Llyn	lake
Llys	court, palace
Maen	stone
Maes	field
Mawr/fawr	big
Melin/felin	mill
Moel/foel	bare hill
Morfa	marsh
Mur	wall
Mynydd/fynydd	mountain
Nant	stream
Neuadd	hall
Newydd	new
Ogof	cave

Pandy	fulling mill
Pant	hollow
Parc	park, field
Pen	head, top
Pentir	headland
Pentre	village
Pistyll	spout, cataract
Plas	mansion
Pont	bridge
Pwll	pool
Rhaeadr	waterfall
Rhiw	hill
Rhos	moorland
Rhyd	ford
Sarn	causeway, road
Siglen	bog, swamp
Tafarn	inn
Tan	under
Tir	land
Tomen	mound
Traeth	beach
Tref	town
Trwyn	promontory
Ty	house
Tyddyn	small farm
Uchaf	upper
Uwch	above, higher
Y, yr	the
Yn	in
Ynys	island
Ysgol	school
Ysgubor	barn
Ystrad	valley floor

1. Welshpool

Route: A stretch of canal towpath and Powis Castle Park feature on this easy walk which has the option of a visit to the castle and its gardens. This is not a walk for dogs – dogs are not allowed in Powis Castle Park.

Distance: 4½ miles.

How to get there: Welshpool is on the A458, west of Shrewsbury.

Public Transport: Welshpool is on the Cambrian main line with trains from Birmingham and Shrewsbury. Buses from Shrewsbury, Oswestry and other nearby towns.

Start: Car park near the Tourist Information Centre.

Map: Explorer 216.

Situated in the valley of the River Severn, Welshpool is a pleasant borderlands town with broad streets and many historic buildings. The name was originally 'Pool' and 'Welsh' was added in the early 19th century to avoid confusion with the English town of Poole. The Welsh name is Trallwng. A charter was granted in 1263 by Gwenwynwyn, Prince of Powis. St Mary's Church dates from the 13th century and has several monuments to the Earls of Powis. Opposite the church door is the stone called Maen Llog which is said to be part of the abbot's chair brought from the medieval abbey of Strata Marcella.

Near the church is Grace Evans' cottage. She was a maid to the Countess of Nithsdale, the daughter of the Earl of Powis. The Earl of Nithsdale was condemned to death and imprisoned in the Tower of London for his part in the 1715 Jacobite Rebellion. The Countess, with the help of other women, smuggled her husband out of the tower dressed in women's clothes. Grace Evans helped in the escape and, as an expression of their gratitude, the Nithsdales gave Grace Evans this cottage.

Welshpool has the only cockpit in Wales on its original site. It was used from the early 18th century until 1849 when cockfighting became illegal. The town has a wide range of architecture with most of the oldest buildings in the High Street. One 17th-century building is said to have been built by the first 'Jones'. Built in 1837, the Town Hall has an indoor market.

The Tea Shops

On this walk you have the option of refreshments en route and/or at the end of the walk.

The tea room at Powis Castle is located in the courtyard and may be visited separately from the castle and garden. A wide variety of hot home-made dishes, including soups, is on offer. The selection of cakes includes Welsh cakes and bara brith. In hot weather you may like to try the home-made lemonade. Open 1.00pm until 5.00pm from the end of March until early November but closed on Mondays and Tuesdays. In July and August it is open daily except for Mondays (open on Bank Holiday Mondays). Tel: 01938 551920.

In Welshpool, you may like to visit Peppers Coffee Shop which has a courtyard with outdoor tables in Puzzle Square. The menu includes baked potatoes, sandwiches and a delicious selection of home-made cakes. Open 9.00am to 5.00pm Mondays to Saturdays. During the summer months also open on Sundays. Tel: 01938 555146.

The Walk

1. At the Tourist Information Centre, cross the road and turn left on a path which runs alongside the car park. Cross the bridge over the canal and, after descending the steps, bear left beside the canal.

   In the late 18th century, a scheme of waterways was planned to link the Severn, Dee and Mersey rivers. The Montgomeryshire Canal Act was authorised in 1794 and the first section, from Welsh Frankton to Llanymynech, opened two years later. The following year the canal passed through Welshpool on its way to Garthmyl which was its terminus until 1821 when the canal finally reached Newtown. Coal, timber, limestone, grain and dairy produce were some of the goods transported. The canal-side at Welshpool was lined with wharves and warehouses. Although road and rail transport soon took over, the Montgomeryshire Canal survived until 1936 when the banking was breached near Welsh Frankton. A short stretch is navigable near Welshpool.

2. Go under a road and pass a lock. Immediately after passing a

The Montgomeryshire Canal

footbridge, have a hedge on your left and the canal on your right. Follow the path for over a kilometre to a footbridge. Cross the footbridge and follow the towpath under the road. Walk on beside the canal to Belan Locks. After passing under the lane, cross the bridge. Immediately bear right to climb a stile near a gate.

3. Walk uphill alongside trees to a stile at a gate. Continue beside a left-hand fence and go downhill to a gate. (Ignore the stile on your left.) Follow a track to a fence and walk uphill to a stile and gate.

4. Cross the lane and take Powis Castle drive. It passes beside the gardens to give a glimpse of the castle. Follow the drive around to the left and bear right at a building to pass the Dairy Pool. Ducks and coots may be present. In about another 100 metres, you will reach a fork. The walk bears right here but, if you wish to visit Powis Castle, garden or tea room, go left to the car park and castle entrance.

The origins of Powis Castle are confused but it is thought

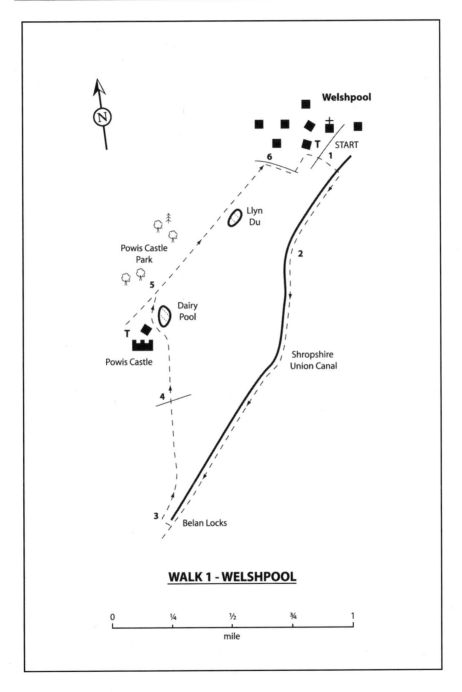

WALK 1 - WELSHPOOL

that the building of the present castle was started in the 13th century by Gruffudd ap Gwenwynwyn and his son Owain. Owain adopted the Norman name de la Pole and the castle passed into the hands of the Cherleton family after the marriage of his daughter Hawys de la Pole to a Norman knight, John de Cherleton. In 1587 the castle was acquired by Sir Edward Herbert who made many alterations and built the long gallery. The Herberts garrisoned the castle for the Royalists when Civil War broke out, but it was taken by Parliamentary forces in 1644. After the Restoration, more rebuilding took place including the grand staircase and state bedroom. The heiress Henrietta Herbert married Edward, the son of Clive of India, and many of Clive's mementoes and possessions were brought to the castle. Powis Castle was bequeathed to the National Trust in 1952. There is a fine collection of paintings and furniture as well as the Clive Museum. Do not miss the famous gardens. The terraces were laid out at the end of the 17th century and the yew trees date from the original planting.

5. Continuing on the walk, follow the drive through Powis Castle Park to a gate and cattle grid. Pass above Llyn Du and, at the end of the drive, leave the park by a gate in the wall and walk up a road to the A548 in Welshpool.

6. Turn right to pass the Town Hall and, in about another 80 metres go left along Hopkins Passage to Peppers Coffee Shop in Puzzle Square. On leaving the coffee shop, go left to a road and the start of the walk.

2. Montgomery

Route: A short walk taking in easy climbs to the castle ruins and the site of an Iron Age hill fort. Dogs are not allowed in the castle grounds.

Distance: 2½ miles.

How to get there: Montgomery is on the B4386 between Shrewsbury and Newtown.

Public Transport: Buses from Shrewsbury and Newtown.

Start: Montgomery Town Square.

Map: Explorer 216.

Lying beneath the ruins of its medieval castle, Montgomery is an attractive, small borderland town with several Georgian buildings. The castle was built in 1223, during the reign of Henry III, to replace an earlier Norman motte and bailey castle, Hen Domen, which lies about one mile north, near the River Severn. Four years later, Montgomery was granted a charter and, eventually, a wall with four gates and a ditch enclosed the town. The main thoroughfare is Broad Street, where markets were held. The imposing Town Hall dates from the 18th century when it was built to replace an earlier half-timbered market hall. In Arthur Street there are buildings dating from the 16th century.

The Castle Kitchen

The Tea Shop

The Castle Kitchen is an early 17th-century building in The Square. Hot lunches, soup, baked potatoes, salads, sandwiches, cakes and cream teas are on offer. At the front of the building, a speciality shop sells organic produce, local honey, cheeses and preserves. There is a pretty, secluded tea garden as well as the cosy tea room. Open on Mondays 10.00am to 5.00pm, Tuesdays 9.30am to 5.00pm, Wednesdays to Saturdays 9.00am to 5.00pm, Sundays 12.00 noon to 5.00pm. Open for evening meals on Fridays and Saturdays. Open all year. Tel: 01686 668795.

The Walk

1. In the Square, face the Town Hall and bear right to pass it on your left. In about 80 metres, go left at an entrance to gardens. Walk beside a wall to a kissing gate and follow the path uphill. Emerge at the site of Montgomery Castle.

> The castle consisted of a series of wards protected by deep ditches. Only fragments of the stronghold remain, but still standing are the twin towers of the gatehouse to the inner ward and a larger tower that contains the 220ft well. The castle survived attacks by the Welsh in the early 13th century and, during Edward I's campaign, the town walls were rebuilt in stone and the castle was re-fortified. During the following years, the castle played a manorial rather than a military role. It passed to the Mortimers and, in the 16th century, to the Herbert family. The sons of Richard Herbert were born in the castle. Edward (born 1583) became known as Lord Herbert of Chirbury whilst his younger brother George (born 1593) was a religious poet. Between 1622 and 1625, Edward built a half-timbered mansion in the middle ward of the castle. During the Civil War, in 1664, the castle surrendered to the Parliamentarians and, five years later, both the mansion and the castle were demolished.

2. After looking around the castle ruins, return to the point where you arrived at the ruins. Do not take the descending path, but take a wider level path that runs above it. After emerging at a car park, walk out to a lane.

3. Turn right on the lane and walk uphill. In 600 metres, at a 1 in 5 road sign, go right and walk uphill through the field to a stile in a right-hand fence. Follow the path through the ditches of the hill fort.

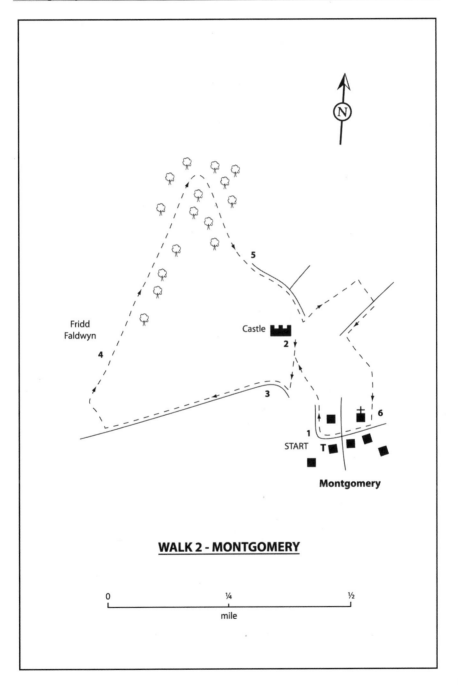

Fridd
Faldwyn

Castle

START

Montgomery

WALK 2 - MONTGOMERY

0   ¼   ½

mile

Excavations that took place between 1937 and 1939 on
Ffridd Faldwyn uncovered several stages of building the Iron
Age hill fort. The earliest phase was a small enclosure protected by a timber palisade with an entrance to the south.
During the next phase, the same enclosure had a timber ram-
part and ditches. At a later date, more ramparts were built
at a lower level. Several round hut sites were uncovered on the
terrace between the enclosures.

4.   Go over the top of the hill and descend the path through decidu-
ous woodland. Pass a fence corner and emerge in a field. Follow
a path to a stile and cross the road to a pavement and turn right.

5.   Ignore the road on the left to Welshpool but, a little further on,
go left down Goal Road. At its end go right on a path to a housing
estate. Emerge on a road and turn right. Take a path on the left
and walk uphill to join another then turn right to pass the school
on your left. Continue ahead to pass the church.

Dating from the 13th century, the church of St Nicholas has
many interesting features. The nave has a timber roof, and a
screen brought from Chirbury Priory at the Dissolution. There
is a superb canopied tomb of Richard Herbert and his wife
with the kneeling figures of their eight children. Nearby are
two recumbent effigies. One is of Sir Edward Mortimer, the
other is a member of the Herbert family. In the churchyard, a
spot known as the Robber's Grave is said to be the resting
place of John Davies who was hanged for sheep stealing in
1821. Protesting his innocence, he prophesied that, if he was
innocent, no grass would grow on his grave for a hundred
years. Apparently, his prophecy came true.

6.   Follow the road as it bears right to The Square, tea shop and start
of the walk.

3. Newtown

Route: A long, but gentle, climb taking in a section of the Severn Way, a way-marked long distance trail. The return to the start is along lanes and field paths. There are extensive views throughout most of the walk.

Distance: 8 miles.

How to get there: Newtown is on the A483, south of Welshpool.

Public Transport: Newtown is on the Cambrian main line with trains from Birmingham and Shrewsbury. Buses from Shrewsbury, Machynlleth and other nearby towns.

Start: Car park near the junction of the A483 and A489 on the east side of the town.

Map: Explorer 215.

Located in a rich, agricultural district on the banks of the River Severn, Newtown is actually quite an old town. In 1279, the Marcher lord Roger de Mortimer was granted a charter for a market in Llanfair Cedewain. The name Newtown came into use in the 1320s and both names were used until the early 19th century. The area became an important centre for the woollen trade, which at first was a cottage industry with the carding, spinning and weaving carried out in cottages and farmhouses. The cloth was taken to England by packhorse. At the end of the 18th century, new types of machinery were introduced and Newtown became an important textile centre. The population grew from about 1000 in 1800 to over 4000 in the early 1830s. Weavers lived in small back-to-back cottages on the lower floors of tall buildings. The upper floors were workshops.

The opening of the Montgomery Canal in 1821 linked Newtown with the national canal system, and other markets. A flannel market was established in the town in 1832, replacing an earlier one at Welshpool and a local landowner, William Pugh, built the Newtown to Llandrindod road (now the A483). A Newtown draper, Pryce Jones, began the first mail order business in the world, based on Welsh flannel. New factories were built, but the industry gradually declined because of the enormous competition from textile towns in

Lancashire and Yorkshire. Many people left the area to work in England.

Robert Owen, a famous socialist, was born in Newtown in 1771. His father was a saddler and ironmonger whilst his mother was the daughter of a local farmer. After a short education at school in Newtown, he left home at the age of ten to become an apprentice in England. By the age of twenty, he was the manager of a Manchester cotton mill. Three years later, he was part owner and manager of New Lanark Mills in Scotland where he established a model industrial village with pleasant working conditions, cheap good housing, a free medical service, a school for infants and a savings bank. He also set up a co-operative settlement at New Harmony in the USA. At the end of his life, he returned to Newtown where he died in 1858 at the age of eighty-seven. There is a museum dedicated to his memory in Broad Street.

The Tea Shop

The Bank Cottage Tea Rooms are in a row of picturesque 16th-century cottages near Robert Owen's memorial garden. There is an

Bank Cottage Tea Rooms

outdoor eating area. On offer are main meals, tasty soups, sand-wiches and a good selection of cakes and pastries. Open 9.00am to 5.00pm Monday to Saturday. Tel: 01686 625771.

The Walk

1. Leave the car park by the exit opposite the post office and imme-diately bear right to pass the memorial garden to Robert Owen on your left. Pass the Bank Cottage Tea Rooms on your left and, after passing a parking area, take a path in the direction of a foot-bridge. Do not cross but bear left to have the River Severn on your right. Pass the old parish church of St Mary.

    St Mary's Church served the parish from the 13th century un-til the 1850s but it is now a shell with only the towers intact. Because of regular occurrences of flooding, another church, St David's, was built in New Road for the congregation. The ruin of St Mary's Church contains Robert Owen's tomb and the mausoleum of the Pryce family of Newtown Hall. Sir John Pryce, who was born in 1698 and married three times, is re-membered for his eccentricity. He did not bury his first two wives after they died, but had them embalmed and kept them in his bedroom. His third wife refused to marry him until they were removed to the family vault.

2. On reaching the next bridge over the river (Long Bridge), go down steps and bear left under the bridge. In about 300 metres, bear right over a footbridge. At a junction of paths, turn right on the path near the river and follow it up to a road. Turn left and, in about 150 metres, go right up steps on an enclosed path. On reaching a road, cross directly to another path bordered by trees.

3. Cross a stile into woodland and take the main path to a stile near a gate. Follow the right boundary of the field to a corner stile. Slant slightly left to a stile in the left-hand hedge. Continue beside the right boundary of the field to a corner stile. Follow the left-hand boundary of the next two fields and then cross the middle of a field to the next stile. Go slightly left to a stile and lane.

4. Cross the lane to another stile and slant right to a stile in the right-hand descending fence. Slant down the field to a gate near

a telegraph pole then follow the right-hand hedge of two fields. Cross over a track to a stile and go slightly left to a stile in the left-hand fence. Descend slightly right through the field in the direction of the nearest buildings. On reaching a fence, take an enclosed path downhill towards Rhydfelin Baptist Church. Follow the access road to a lane.

5. Turn right and, in 200 metres, cross a stile on the left. Follow the right-hand boundary of the field to have Fachwen Pool on your right. Keep above the trees and cross a stile at the top edge of woodlands. In about 120 metres, climb a stile on the right to take a path beside the lake.

6. In a few metres, after crossing a stream, leave the lake to cross a stile in the fence. Pass through trees to emerge in a field and follow the right-hand fence to a stile in the top right-hand corner. Descend to a small footbridge and walk up to a stile. Slant slightly left uphill through the field to a way-marked post. From here are wide views over the surrounding countryside. Turn left and cross a stile at a gate and walk on uphill beside the right-hand fence. Descend to a stile at a gate and walk along a shady track above a valley.

7. Emerge on a lane and bear right to another. Turn right (soon leaving the Severn Way) and follow the lane to a junction. Go right again and follow this lane to another junction. Bear right then go immediately left on a dead end lane.

8. In 400 metres, just before a left bend in the lane, cross a stile on the right. Go slightly left to follow the left boundary of this field to a stile in the far-left corner. Walk on close to the left-hand fence (can be muddy here) to cross a corner stile and another nearby. Walk uphill beside the right-hand fence to a stile in the top right-hand corner. Bear right through a gap into the next field and walk uphill along the right edge of the field. Shortly after passing a pond in a field on the right, cross a stile and plank bridge on the right. Walk on beside the left-hand hedge to a corner stile.

9. Turn right on the lane and, in a few paces, go left on another. Follow this lane for just over a mile until meeting the 30 mph sign at the edge of Newtown. In another 30 metres go right on a

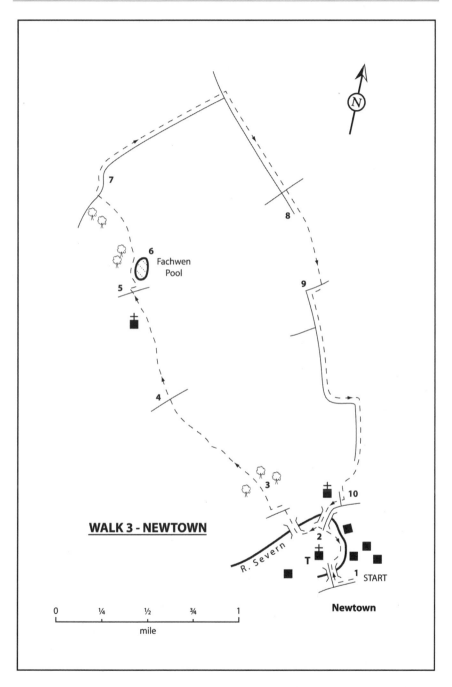

N

7

8

9

6 Fachwen
Pool

5

4

3

10

2

T

1 START

WALK 3 - NEWTOWN

R. Severn

Newtown

| 0 | ¼ | ½ | ¾ | 1 |

mile

path between hedges. On reaching a road, cross directly and walk downhill to emerge on a main road.

10. Turn right to pass the Textile Museum. At a roundabout, go left across Long Bridge. After crossing the River Severn, turn left and retrace your steps past the old church to Bank Cottage Tea Rooms and the car park.

4. Llanidloes

Route: A moderate walk, with superb views, that follows tracks and lanes in the countryside around the Clywedog and Severn valleys.

Distance: 6 miles.

How to get there: Lying south-west of Newtown, Llanidloes is on the A470 about half-way between Dolgellau and Builth Wells.

Public Transport: Buses from Shrewsbury, Newtown, Aberystwyth and Rhayader.

Start: Llanidloes, the Old Market Hall.

Map: Explorer 214.

Llanidloes lies at the confluence of the Clywedog and Severn rivers. This small town derives its name from St Idloes who founded a church here in the 7th century. The present church, with its 14th-century tower and wooden belfry, sits close to the Severn Porte where the two rivers merge. The half-timbered market hall in the centre of the town was built about 1600 and is the only surviving building of its kind in Wales. Markets were held on the open lower cobbled floor and John Wesley preached here in the 18th century.

The town was an important centre for the flannel industry in the early 19th century, but low wages and poor harvests encouraged interest in Chartism. This movement took its name from the People's Charter of 1838, which had a six-point plan for parliamentary reform. It demanded votes for all men, the right to vote by secret ballot, annually elected parliaments, payment of MPs, abolition of their property qualifications and equal electoral districts. Hetherington, a leader of the movement, toured the flannel towns of mid Wales in 1839 to talk about the movement. Some weavers in Llanidloes adopted the Charter and collected firearms by stealing them from local farms. Several local constables were enlisted and three policemen came from London to deal with the riots. They arrested three of the Chartist leaders but they were released by local weavers. The Chartists ruled for several days until the arrival of the Montgomeryshire Yeomanry. Of the thirty-two people arrested, three men were transported to Australia.

Llanidloes: the old market hall

The Tea Shop

The cosy Cobblers Tea Room is located in a conservation area in the High Street. The building has been a pub, furniture emporium and a shoe shop and cobblers. The varied menu includes home-made soups and main meals, salads, sandwiches, home-made cakes, bara brith, Welsh teas and cream teas. Open 10.00am until 5.00pm Monday to Saturday. Opens on Sundays for bookings. Tel: 01686 413173.

The Walk

1. From the Market Hall, walk down Long Bridge Street. Bear left at the roundabout to cross the bridge and immediately bear left along the road for Llyn Clywedog.

2. In about 900 metres, go left along a dead end lane. Pass Clywedog Holiday Homes Park and walk uphill. On reaching a fork, go left downhill and, in about 100 metres, go left on a track to pass a ruin on the left. Follow it to a footbridge spanning the River Clywedog.

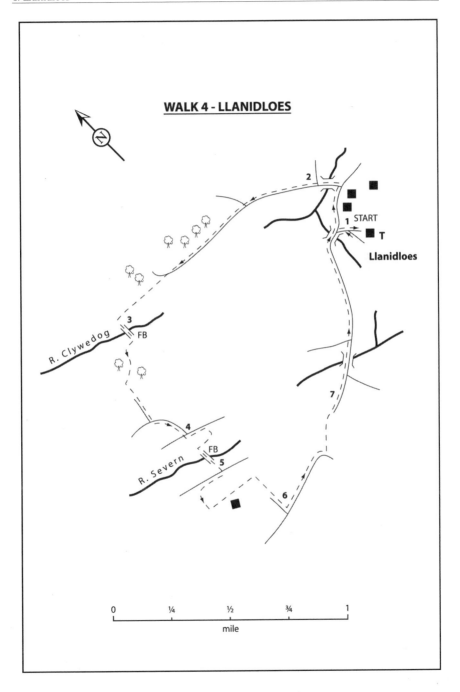

WALK 4 - LLANIDLOES

N

2

1 START

T

Llanidloes

R. Clywedog

3

FB

4

R. Severn

FB

5

7

6

0   ¼   ½   ¾   1

mile

3. Cross the bridge and follow a path uphill through the trees. In
    about 350 metres, it bears left to a gate. On reaching a junction,
    go right uphill. Go through a gate and around a left bend. The
    lane passes alongside fields and descends to a junction. Bear left
    to emerge on a road at Glan-y-nant.

4. Turn left and, in about 100 metres, cross a stile on the right near
    a gate and drive. Descend a few metres through the field then go
    left and shortly have trees and a fence on the right. Cross a stile
    and bear right along an access lane. After passing the last house,
    follow a path downhill to a footbridge across the River Severn.
    On the far side of the river, take a path slightly left and go
    through a gate. Veer left to walk uphill along the left boundary of
    the field to a stile and lane.

5. Turn right along the lane to pass a farm drive on the right. Walk
    uphill and, in about another 50 metres, go through a gate on the
    left. Follow a track uphill through the trees to a gate. Walk ahead
    to reach another path and turn left. In 200 metres, go through a
    gate on the left to join a track. Pass a building on the left and
    follow an enclosed track to a gate near a farmhouse. Continue
    along the farm access lane and follow it around to the right.
    Walk uphill and shortly descend to a lane junction.

6. Turn left. In about 700 metres, the lane curves right. Just beyond
    the bend, go through a gate on the left. Slant to the left and walk
    steeply downhill through the field towards the lower corner of
    woodland. Go through a gate at the corner and bear slightly right
    to a stile.

7. Turn right along the lane to a junction and then bear left across
    Felindre Bridge. Walk uphill to another junction and turn right.
    In about a kilometre, bear right across Shortbridge over the
    River Severn. Walk uphill to the start at the Old Market Hall in
    Llanidloes. To visit the Cobblers Tea Room, walk ahead along
    Great Oak Street, and turn right into High Street. The tea room is
    on the right.

5. Rhayader

Route: A varied, easy walk following paths, tracks, lanes and a former railway track.

Distance: 4¼ miles.

How to get there: Rhayader is on the A470, north of Builth Wells.

Public Transport: Buses from Llandrindod Wells and Llanidloes.

Start: Car park near the Leisure Centre (on the A470).

Map: Explorer 200.

Rhayader is a small, pleasant livestock market town on the east bank of the River Wye. A castle was built above the river in the 12th century by Lord Rhys of Deheubarth. It was attacked and taken several times by opposing sides before being burnt in 1231 by forces of Llywelyn ap Iorwerth. Five hundred years later, skeletons believed to be of the slain garrison were found laid in neat rows when a new church was being built.

This part of mid Wales remained a wild place. In the early 16th century, an assize judge visited Rhayader alternately with New Radnor. One Sunday, a few days prior to a captured bandit being tried, other robbers killed the judge when he was on his way to church. They were captured and hanged but the courts were moved to Presteigne.

For hundreds of years, drovers brought their cattle, sheep and other livestock through Rhayader on their way to English markets. They generally covered about 15 miles a day at a steady speed of two miles an hour. When the turnpike roads were set up, drovers tried to avoid the Rhayader tollgate by driving the cattle through the River Wye. Many farmers and others resented the turnpike system and this anger resulted in the Rebecca Riots of the 1840s. The name Rebecca was taken from Genesis and the gangs called themselves Rebecca's Daughters. They disguised themselves by wearing women's clothing and horse-hair wigs. The rioters attacked and burnt the tollgates at night and, as soon as the tollgates were replaced, they destroyed them again. Rhayader, being at a crossroads of turnpike routes, was one of the main centres for the riots. Tollgates gradually disappeared and eventually County Councils

The River Wye near Rhayader

took over the responsibility for the roads. In the meantime, Rebecca's Daughters continued their lawless ways by poaching salmon in defiance of Fishery Laws.

The Tea Shop

Situated near the clock at the crossroads, Carole's Cake Shop and Old Swan Tearooms are in the oldest house in Rhayader. The cosy tearoom has an original oak panelled wall dating from the 17th century. The varied menu includes main meals, jacket potatoes, soup, home-made cakes and scones, Welsh tea and cream teas. Open 9.00am until 5.00pm Monday to Saturday but closes at 2.30pm on Thursdays. Open 11.00am to 5.00pm on most Sundays. Open all year. Tel: 01597 811060.

The Walk

1. From the car park, bear right to pass the Leisure Centre on the left. Cross the road at the traffic lights and walk ahead along a lane. Cross directly over a crossroads to Castle Road. At its end go through a small gate on the left to the site of Rhayader Castle.

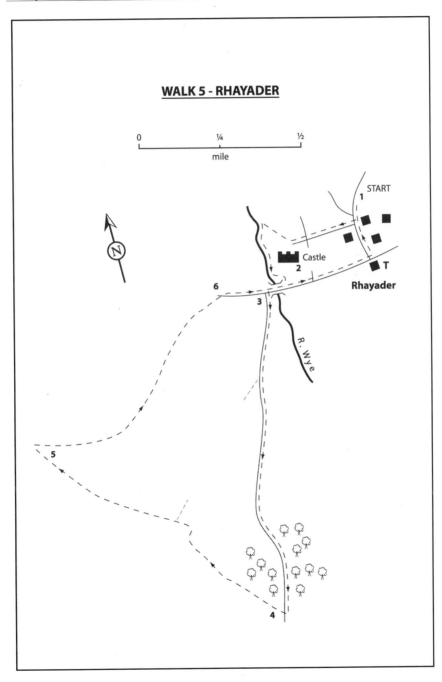

WALK 5 - RHAYADER

Rhayader Castle was built in 1177 by Lord Rhys of Deheubarth. He rebuilt it in 1194 before it was captured by the sons of Cadwallon ap Madog of Maelienydd, a nearby kingdom. Shortly afterwards, it was lost to Roger Mortimer but recaptured by the Welsh in 1202. The only visible remains of the castle are the ditches.

2. Return through the gate and go left through another to walk downhill to the River Wye. Turn left at a junction to follow the Riverside Walk. The path passes beside cliffs before emerging at a lane end. Walk out to a road and bear right. After crossing the bridge over the river, go left on a lane.

3. Walk uphill along the lane and ignore a track on the right. Continue along the lane and pass through some woodland. At the end of the trees on the right, bear right on a track to have woods on your right and a hedge on the left.

4. Follow the track slightly downhill and around bends to a gate. Pass farm buildings and arrive at a track junction. Cross by bearing slightly left to a gate and enclosed track. Continue beside a fence and go through another gate. Pass some houses and, a few metres before reaching a road, turn right through a small gate onto a surfaced path.

The path forms a section of the Elan Valley Trail, a walkers' and cyclists' route along the trackbed of the former standard gauge railway line between Craig Coch Dam and Cwmdauddwr near Rhayader. The line was built to carry building materials for the construction of the Birmingham Corporation dams in the Elan Valley. Work started on the railway in 1893. Along the trail you will pass the Elan Valley Junction where the railway joined the Mid Wales Valley Line which was part of the Cambrian Railway. Further on, you will pass the old railway tunnel. It was purchased by the Radnorshire Wildlife Trust to protect bats which hibernate in its crevices. Some of the line to the north and south of the tunnel is also part of the reserve and flowers such as eyebright and willow-herb grow here. Birds that may be spotted include tree sparrow and grey wagtail.

5. Follow the path through gates and pass the old railway junction and tunnel. Walk downhill to emerge on a road.

6. Turn right through Cwmdauddwr. Cross the bridge over the River Wye and walk uphill to a junction of roads near the clock. Carole's Old Swan Tearooms are on the right. Turn left to return to the car park and start of the walk.

6. Elan Valley

Route: A lovely, varied walk around the Caban-coch Reservoir following moorland and forest tracks. Some climbing.

Distance: 7½ miles.

How to get there: From Rhayader take the B4518 through Elan Village to the Visitor Centre.

Public Transport: Post bus from Rhayader.

Start: Elan Valley Visitor Centre car park.

Map: Explorer 200.

Known as 'The Lake District of Mid Wales', the Elan Valley Reservoirs are famous for their magnificent scenery. They were built in the late 19th century to provide Birmingham with clean water for its growing population. The area was chosen because of its high rainfall, narrow valleys that were easy to dam and the high altitude. The water could travel by gravity the 73 miles to Birmingham. A parliamentary act was passed in 1892 for the compulsory purchase of the catchment area and the building of a series of dams which drowned eighteen farmhouses, a church and a school. Landowners received compensation but ordinary people received nothing and many emigrated. The large numbers of workers employed in the construction of the dams were mainly from outside the area. After being deloused and medically examined, the navvies were billeted in a wooden hut village which had two hospitals, one for injuries and the other for infectious diseases.

A narrow-gauge railway line was constructed to link the work site with Rhayader. From Elan village additional branches were laid out to the base of each dam. Much of the building work was done manually and there were many accidents. The River Elan dams (Caban-coch, Garreg-ddu, Penygarreg and Craig Goch) were opened in 1904 by Edward VII and Queen Alexandra. The large Claerwen dam, completed in 1952 and opened by Elizabeth II, doubles the capacity of the reservoirs. Caban-coch reservoir is too low for the extraction of water by gravity. After heavy rain, water flows over the 122ft dam. Water for Birmingham is extracted at the Foel Tower on the Carreg-ddu reservoir. The wooden hut accommodation was

Caban-coch reservoir

replaced by a stone house village. Completed in 1909, it housed workers employed by the water authority and had a school and a chapel.

In front of the Visitor Centre is a sculpture of Percy Bysshe Shelley who visited his cousin Thomas Grove at Cwm Elan in 1811 after being expelled from Oxford. He returned with his young wife Harriet and they stayed at a house called Nantgwyllt which is now submerged under the waters of Caban-coch reservoir. Shelley had hoped to buy the house and set it up as a House of Meditation where he, his wife and the philosopher Godwin and others could live in harmony. His plans came to nothing as the price was too high and he was soon estranged from Harriet. His second wife was Mary Godwin who, as Mary Shelley, wrote 'Frankenstein'.

In the 12th century, the monks of Strata Florida were given upland grazing rights as far as Rhayader by Lord Rhys, ruler of South Wales. They introduced sheep farming on a large scale but much of the area around the Elan Valley remained sessile oak woodlands until after the Middle Ages. Coniferous trees have been planted around some of the reservoirs but there is now a programme to replace these with oak and other broadleaved trees. Some ancient sessile oak woods remain on the steep hillsides and these are frequented by pied flycatcher, redstart and wood warbler. In the coniferous plantations look out for goldcrest, siskin and crossbill. A condition of the Act of Parliament in 1892 was to allow the right of access for recreation in the Elan Valley and the whole area has become popular with bird-watchers, walkers and cyclists.

The Tea Shop

In the Elan Valley Visitor Centre you will find a self-service café as well as exhibitions and a shop. The building was originally the main workshop for the building of the dams. It became a visitor centre in 1985 and was enlarged in 1997. The café offers hot dishes, soup, salads, jacket potatoes, baps and various cakes. There is an outdoor eating area. Open 10.00am until 5.30pm daily from mid March to the end of October. Tel: 01597 810899.

The Walk

1. From the Visitor Centre, walk towards Caban-coch dam. Go through a gate and walk ahead to pass the turbine house. Bear left around it and cross a bridge. On the other side, go right, then left and right again to ascend a long, stepped path. Go through a small gate at the top and bear right to the dam.

2. With Caban-coch reservoir on your right, follow a clear level path through the heather. At the end of the level area, the path descends a little and becomes narrow. In about 150 metres, go left on a stepped path to a stile in a fence. Bear right on a path to enter woodland. The reservoir is below on your right. Cross another stile and follow the path as it bears left above the remains of the Nant y Gro dam.

     The Nant y Gro dam was blown up during the 1939 to 1945 war. Because of its remoteness and the fact that it was of the same design as the Ruhr dams, though smaller, it was used to develop the 'bouncing bombs' used in the Dambusters raid in 1943.

3. Walk uphill away from the reservoir. Pass a plantation and a corner fence then continue uphill through bracken towards coniferous trees. Bear right in front of the trees and walk down-

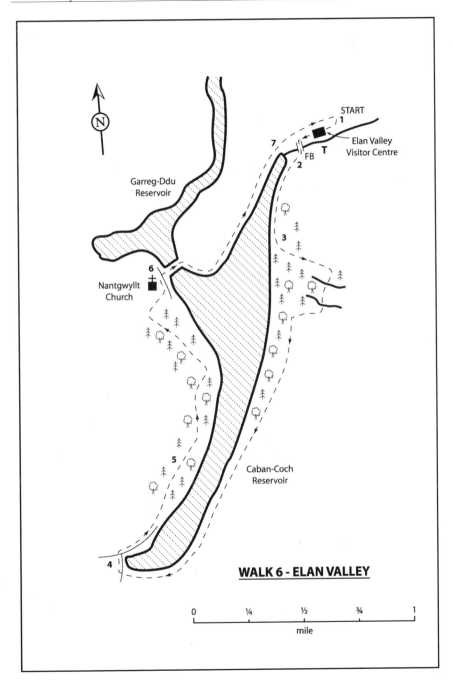

WALK 6 - ELAN VALLEY

hill to cross two streams. On reaching the edge of the forest, keep the fence on your right. Ignore a gate into the forest, and walk on with the trees on your right. Follow the track downhill and across two streams. After joining a lesser track coming in from the right, walk ahead to ford a stream and go through a gate. Pass an old farmhouse on the left and maintain your direction.

4. Cross a bridge and walk up to a road. Turn right and, in about 300 metres, you will see a small parking area on the left. From behind the information board, take a path that slants uphill. At a fork, go right on a path and pass through a gate into forest.

5. Follow a path through the trees and join a track. Continue ahead and, after crossing a stream, you will reach a junction of tracks. Ignore the track to the left (to Penglaneinon Farm) and to the right (to the road) and walk ahead on a fairly level track. In just over a kilometre from the track junction and a few metres before reaching a stream, go right at a way-marked post and follow a track downhill. Go through a gate and turn left at the lane. To your left is Nantygwyllt Church.

6. Bear right across the bridge. On your left is Garreg-ddu reservoir and the Foel tower. On reaching a road junction, turn right on a permissive path that runs above Caban-coch reservoir.

7. After passing through a gate at the Caban-coch dam, walk on along the Elan Valley Trail. In about 400 metres, descend steps on the right to the car park, Visitor Centre and café.

7. Llandrindod Wells

Route: A fascinating, varied walk visiting a lake, attractive woodlands, an ancient church and the Rock Park Spa.

Distance: 6½ miles.

How to get there: Llandrindod Wells is on the A483, south of Newtown and north of Builth Wells.

Public Transport: Llandrindod Wells is on the Heart of Wales line. Trains from Shrewsbury and Swansea. Buses from Rhayader and Builth Wells.

Start: Tourist Information Centre in Temple Street.

Map: Explorer 200.

The Romans discovered the mineral waters at Llandrindod Wells but it was the 18th century before the town was developed as a spa. Exploitation of the springs began in 1736 when a local woman, Mrs Jenkins, used the saline waters to cure ulcers on her daughters head. She healed other local people with various ailments, and the fame of the waters spread after a poem appeared in the Gentleman's Magazine:

'Let England boast Bath's crowded springs
Llandrindod happier, Cambria sings.'

The beneficial effects of the waters were compared favourably with the European spas. In the mid 18th century, a Mr Grosvenor of Shrewsbury built a hotel near the old parish church on the hill above the lake. Many visitors came, but not just for the waters. A racecourse had opened and soon the place had such notoriety for its gambling and drunkenness that, in 1787, the hotel was closed. Llandrindod declined although, in 1817, Dr Williams of Aberystwyth published a pamphlet about the medicinal benefits of the springs.

After the arrival of the railway in 1866, Llandrindod grew rapidly. In the space of forty years, the town's population of less than 350 in 1871 rose to almost 2,800 by 1911. From a small village, surrounded by common land, grew a purpose-built fashionable spa town with broad streets, spacious squares and gardens. Pump rooms and bathhouses were built for the thousands of Victorian visitors who came to take the waters for complaints such as rheumatism, anaemia, gout and dyspepsia.

Llandrindod Wells has retained much of its Victorian architecture and character. Every August the town relives its past by holding a week-long Victorian Festival.

The Tea Shop

The Rock Park Spa Restaurant is housed in the old pump room of the spa in tranquil woodlands. Light meals, afternoon teas and an excellent selection of cakes are available. Open 10.00am to 5.00pm Tuesday to Saturday. Evening meals 6.00pm to 9.00pm. Also open for Sunday lunches. Tel: 01597 829267.

The Rock Spa tea room

The Walk

1. With your back to the Tourist Information Centre, go left past the memorial. Pass the Hotel Metropole and, on reaching a small roundabout, go left then, almost immediately, bear right. Walk

uphill and pass the site of Capel Maelog on the left. Continue to the lake.

The lake was a marshy hollow used for the cutting of peat for fuel until the 1860s when the railway brought coal. On the building of the spa town, the lake was dammed to form an attractive boating lake. Here you may see swans, moorhens and various waterfowl.

2. Bear left beside the lake. In about 60 metres, ignore a footpath on the left and pass a house. Ignore a track on the left and continue along the road as it curves to the right. In about another 50 metres take a footpath on the left and follow it uphill through woodland. On reaching a fork, in about 200 metres, go left to join another path then go left again. At first fairly level, the path eventually descends gently to a stile. In just over another 100 metres, ignore a path on the left. Walk on a few paces, then bear slightly left to follow a fence on the left to a stile.

3. Do not cross the stile but bear right on a path uphill, to join another path. Turn left, uphill, and, after coming out of the trees go slightly left to a stile.

    Bear slightly left to a stile near a gate and continue uphill over two more stiles. Climb up to a trig point from where, on clear days, are wide views over the surrounding countryside. Go ahead, downhill, to a stile and lane.

4. Turn left along the lane and ignore a track on the left at a footpath signpost. In another 300 metres, go left over a stile and follow the track ahead. Go through a gate and continue on a clear path through woodlands. Descend to a gate and walk downhill through coniferous trees to emerge on a lane. Turn left and, in a few paces, take a footpath on the right across Shaky Bridge to visit the Church of St Michael.

    Enclosed by a circular churchyard containing yew trees thought to be over 1000 years old, the Church of St Michael dates from the 13th century but has an older foundation. Inside is a Norman font and the remains of a medieval rood screen. The church is in the parish of Cefnllys, once a place of much importance. On top of the hill stood Cefnllys Castle

which was rebuilt several times and may have originally be-
longed to Welsh princes. It is thought that in the 13th century
the Mortimer family built a new castle on the site, but it was
later rebuilt at the southern end of the ridge. By the 16th century, it was in ruins.

5.   From the church, retrace your steps across the River Ithon and
turn right into the nature reserve on the river bank.

Situated on the west bank of the River Ithon, the Bailey Einon
nature reserve is a long strip of mixed broadleaved woodland.
Oak, hazel, ash and alder provide a habitat for woodpecker,
tree creeper, wren, bullfinch, pied flycatcher, chiffchaff and
wood warbler. Otters are occasionally seen in the river.

6.   Immediately, cross a stile on the left and walk directly uphill for
about 150 metres then bear right, continuing uphill, to a stile in
the top boundary of the field. Turn right along the lane and, at a
junction, ignore the lane ahead and bear left. Ignore paths and
tracks leading off the lane until you reach a 30 mph sign at a left
bend.

7.   Bear right and ignore a left fork. Follow a private road and, in
about 50 metres, go left beside a hedge to a stile. Bear right and
walk along a path to a kissing gate and small footbridge. Go
uphill along the right boundary of the field then ahead into the
next field. Go downhill to a kissing gate opposite a house. Turn
left along the farm track and through a gate to walk downhill
between fields. Cross a road and continue downhill to a road
junction. Turn left to the Tourist Information Centre at the start
of the walk.

8.   To visit the Rock Spa Restaurant, turn right and pass Temple
Gardens on the left. Go directly over a road junction and cross a
bridge over the railway. Turn left downhill and cross a road on
the left. Go through the Rock Spa gate and follow a track downhill. At the bottom, go left then right to see the chalybeate spring
then walk ahead to the restaurant.

Several types of spring have been found in the Rock Park.
These include magnesium, sulphur, saline and chalybeate –
the latter containing large amounts of sodium and calcium,

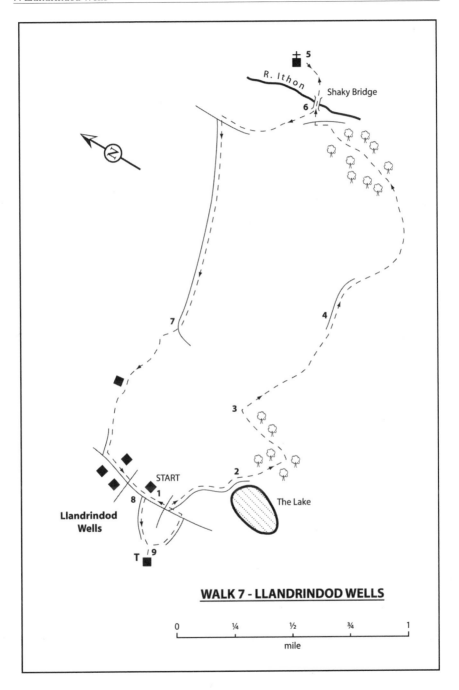

WALK 7 - LLANDRINDOD WELLS

together with iron and other elements. Sulphur was considered helpful for complaints such as skin problems, gastritis and ailments of the bladder and kidneys. Both sulphur and saline were prescribed for gout and rheumatism sufferers. Chalybeate was recommended for anaemia. After one of his family was cured by the chalybeate well, the lord of the manor gave its waters to the public for ever. Cures at the spa often involved drinking saline water before breakfast, sulphur in the morning and afternoon, also chalybeate after meals. Bathing in the waters and other health treatments were prescribed. Entertainments were provided for the invalids.

9.   Retrace your steps past the spring and, in a few paces, go right on a path to have the stream below on your right. Ignore a bridge on your right and continue ahead. Ignore other paths leading off and follow the main path up to the road. Go left to the small roundabout and retrace your steps to the start of the walk.

8. Builth Wells

Route: Field paths beside the River Wye are followed by a walk through the lovely Dunhonw valley and an optional climb to a fine viewpoint.

Distance: 4½ or 6 miles.

How to get there: Builth Wells is on the A483 and A470, north of Brecon.

Public Transport: Buses from Brecon and Llandrindod Wells.

Start: South side of the Wye Bridge, at the junction of the A470 and A483.

Map: Explorer 188.

Builth Wells is at its busiest in late July when the Royal Welsh Show takes place in the Llanelwedd showground on the north side of the River Wye. This agricultural show is the biggest in Wales and attracts huge crowds from a wide area. Two miles west of the town at Cilmeri is a monument to Llywelyn ap Gruffudd (Llywelyn the Last) who was killed nearby in 1282, thus ending Welsh independence. Having failed to raise support from Builth Castle, he had separated from his bodyguard and had only one companion with him when he was surrounded by English soldiers.

Builth was a settlement of about eighty houses when it was destroyed by a great fire in 1691. Money was sent from all over Britain to help rebuild the town. Many present buildings date from the 18th and 19th centuries. Lady Hester Stanhope, niece of the younger William Pitt, visited Builth in 1808 and made excursions on horseback. The following year she returned to stay at Glan Irfon, from where she helped her poorer neighbours. Later she travelled east to Lebanon.

Builth's Welsh name is Llanfair ym Muallt (St Mary's in the cow pasture). Builth is the English spoken 'buellt'. Wells was added when a saline spring was discovered in 1830 and the waters were exploited.

The Tea Shop

You will find the Cosy Corner Tea Rooms in an 18th-century building on a corner of the High Street. The varied menu includes home-made soup, cakes and cream teas. Vegetarian meals are available. Open 10.00am until 5.00pm Monday to Saturday. In the winter it closes at 4.30pm, and 3.00pm on Wednesdays. Tel: 01982 553585.

The Walk

1. At the bridge, face the Lion Hotel and bear left along the A470 in the direction of Brecon. In about 100 metres, turn left at a footpath signpost to have a fence on your right. Pass a building on the left and walk down to a small footbridge and stile. Walk beside the River Wye and, in about 200 metres, join a track. Follow it into a field and, when the track veers away from the river, continue along the river bank. Further on, have some trees on the right and cross a stile. Continue beside the line of trees to the next stile then walk on towards woodlands and a stile about 100 metres to the right of the river.

2. Follow a clear but rough path through the coniferous trees. At a waymarked post take the left-hand path to a stile and field. Continue along the river bank but, about 50 metres before the end of the field, bear right uphill to a stile located 50 metres right of the left corner. Turn left along the grass verge of the A470. In 400 metres, before reaching the bridge over the River Dunhonw, go right through a field gate on to a track.

3. Follow the track ahead. It passes under wires and arrives at a field gate. Go through it and ignore a gate on the right. Walk ahead but, when there is a gate in front of you, bear right and go through another gate. Veer left to have a fence on the left. Walk on through the next gate and, in another 150 metres, pass an old barn on the left.

4. Pass through some trees and then walk beside woodland. Enter a large field and slant to the left downhill to a gate. Walk straight ahead through a gate into another field and pass a small building and a line of trees on the left. Go through a gate on to a track and emerge on a lane. Bear right uphill and, in 300 metres, cross a stile on the right if you wish to make a diversion to the summit of Garth (otherwise skip all the directions before point 6).

5. Walk uphill with a line of trees on your left. Go through a gap and, further on, cross or go through a barrier to have a fence on the left. Pass through a gate and follow the clear path to the

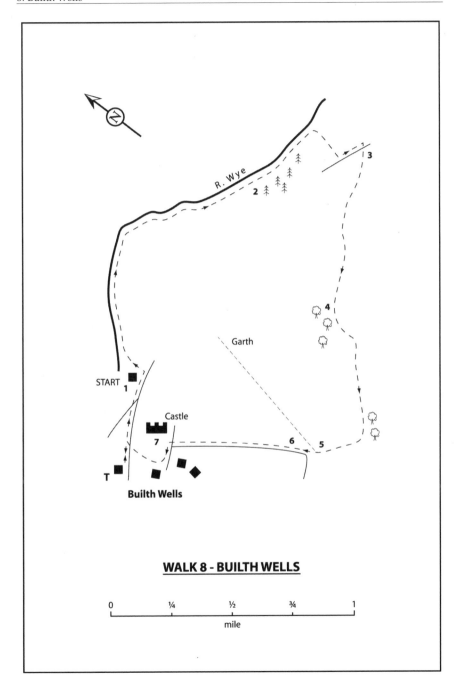

WALK 8 - BUILTH WELLS

0   ¼   ½   ¾   1

mile

summit of Garth. After admiring the views, retrace your steps to the lane and turn right.

6. Join another lane and keep ahead to walk in the direction of Builth Wells. In about a mile, at a road junction, turn left. In 80 metres, bear right along an access lane and, in a few metres, cross a stile on the right. Go left – or right – to walk around the site of Builth Castle.

A motte and bailey castle was built at Builth by de Braose lords in the early 12th century. It was destroyed by Rhys ap Gruffudd of Deheubarth in 1168. Following reconstruction, it later passed to Llywelyn ap Iorwerth when his son Dafydd married Isabella de Braose. After Llywelyn died, the English took the castle and held it for about 18 years until it was besieged by Llywelyn ap Gruffudd. During Edward I's campaign, English forces took the site and built a new castle with a large keep on the motte and walls lower down. John Giffard was constable in 1282 when Llywelyn ap Gruffudd was ambushed and killed near Builth. There was a constable at the castle in 1525 but, shortly afterwards, the fortification was demolished and its stonework used for the building of local mansions.

7. Return over the stile and go left to the road. Turn right and, in about 80 metres, go right downhill to the main street in Builth Wells. Turn left to visit the Cosy Corner Tea Rooms.

9. Llanwrtyd Wells

Route: Good paths and tracks through the delightful Irfon valley with an optional visit to an interesting old church.

Distance: 3½ miles.

How to get there: Llanwrtyd Wells is on the A483, west of Builth Wells and north of Llandovery.

Public Transport: Llanwrtyd Wells is on the Heart of Wales line. Trains from Shrewsbury and Swansea.

Start: Crossroads in Llanwrtyd Wells, at the bridge spanning the River Irfon.

Map: Explorer 187.

A sulphur spring was discovered at Llanwrtyd in 1732 by Reverend Theophilus Evans of Llangammarch. Suffering from chronic scurvy, he had heard of a reputedly poisonous spring. When he found the strong smelling waters, he was reluctant to drink until he saw a cheerful looking frog hop from the depths. After drinking the water daily for two months, he was cured. The spring water became famous because of its high sulphur content, which was said to be the highest in Britain. A well and bathhouses were built and the coming of the railway in the mid 19th century brought many visitors to the spa. A dome-shaped building covers the sulphur spring near the pump house in the park at the former Dol-y-Coed Hotel. Another well was established at Victoria Wells.

Today, Llanwrtyd Wells claims to be the smallest town in Britain. The local area is well known for its variety of outdoor pursuits, which includes bog snorkelling competitions. On the town green there is a remarkable, steel sculpture of a red kite.

The Tea Shop

Situated at the crossroads on a former droving route to England, The Drover's Rest Tea Rooms serves home-made food including delicious cakes, bara brith and Welsh rarebit. Cream teas and Welsh afternoon teas are available. Lunches are served every day and vegetarians are catered for. There is a small tea garden. Open every day from mid morning to 4.30pm or 5.00pm. Tel: 01591 610264.

The Walk

1. From the crossroads, cross the bridge over the Irfon and, in about 100 metres, turn right in the direction of Victoria Wells. In 600 metres, go left on a path to have a fence on the left and a house on the right. Go through a gate and slant to the right as you walk uphill through the field to a gate. Cross a track to reach a right-hand fence and follow a track uphill to a junction.

2. Bear right through a gate and pass a reservoir on the right. Emerge at a lane end and turn right on a green track. Walk down-hill and go through a gate into forest. Ignore paths leading off. Stay on the main track until you meet another track then bear right, downhill. Notice – but do not take – a footpath on the right. Cross a bridge over a stream and continue ahead past Dinas Mill to a crossroads near St David's Church.

> St David's was the parish church until 1896, when the church of St James was built in Llanwrtyd Wells. It is thought that

St David's church

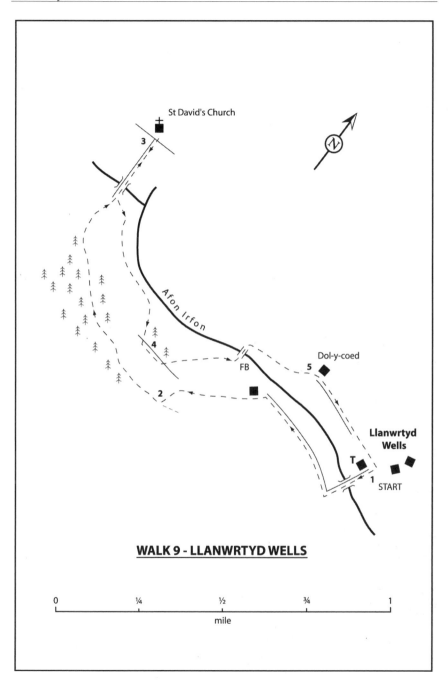

St David's Church

3

Afon Irfon

4

FB

2

Dol-y-coed

5

Llanwrtyd
Wells

T

1

START

WALK 9 - LLANWRTYD WELLS

0	¼	½	¾	1

mile

St David himself founded a church here, but the first building
was probably made of wood. The present church has some medieval features and the porch may be 16th century. Near the
font is a Celtic cross which possibly dates from the founding
of the church. Reverend Theophilus Evans, who discovered the
curative powers of the wells at Llanwrtyd, was vicar of St David's from 1732 to 1767. The church was extensively restored
in 1861.

3. Retrace your steps for 250 metres to the footpath seen earlier and
    pass through the gate. Go slightly right to follow a fence on the
    right. Cross a stile at a gate and bear right to another gate and
    stile near buildings. Pass a house on the left and go left through a
    gate. In about 60 metres, cross a small footbridge over a stream,
    but ignore the bridge on the left across the river. Walk on with
    the river nearby on your left. Cross a stile at some trees and walk
    uphill to reach the lane near Victoria Wells Motel.

4. Turn left and, in a few metres, go left again. Pass through a gate
    and slant down the field towards trees. Enter woodland and
    cross a footbridge over the river. Immediately turn right and go
    through a small gate. Walk up to a track and turn right.

5. Pass Dol-y-Coed on the left and emerge on a road. Turn right and
    follow it to the crossroads at the Drover's Rest Tearooms and
    Restaurant.

10. Tregaron

Route: A fine walk following field paths and lanes with the possibility of seeing the red kite. Some climbing. Short sections of path may be wet.

Distance: 3½ miles.

How to get there: Tregaron is on the A485, south-east of Aberystwyth.

Public Transport: Buses from Aberystwyth and Lampeter.

Start: Tregaron car park, near the Square.

Map: Explorer 199.

The small town of Tregaron lies on a tributary of the River Teifi. Until about 100 years ago, it was a gathering place for drovers as they started off through the Abergwesyn Pass on their long journey to England. George Borrow, the 19th-century author of 'Wild Wales', met a retired drover on his way to Tregaron and, after asking 'What kind of place is Tregaron?', was informed 'Oh, very good place; not quite so big as London, but very good place'. The drover went on to tell Borrow that the town was famous for the exploits of the legendary Twm Shon Catti, a joker and thief who lived in the area in the 16th century. He played pranks such as selling a stolen bull back to its owner after disguising it with a long, false tail. However, after marrying a rich widow, he obtained a pardon and became a justice of the peace, waging war against evildoers.

George Borrow stayed at the Talbot Hotel and in the Square nearby is a statue of Henry Richard, the 'Apostle of Peace', who was born in Tregaron in 1812. He became secretary of the Peace Society in 1848 and organised peace conferences in Brussels and Paris at which the principles of international arbitration to settle disputes were recognised. He became MP for Merthyr Tydfil in 1868 and died twenty years later. So great was his influence, it is thought his ideas formed the basis for the foundation of the later League of Nations.

The Tea Shops

You have a choice of two refreshment stops. In the main Square you will find the unique Rhiannon Celtic Design Centre where outstanding Celtic jewellery, arts and crafts are on display. In the building there is a Welsh Tearoom which serves light refreshments, salads, afternoon teas and traditional Welsh food such as cawl (soup), bara brith and Welsh cakes. Open from 9.00am until 5.30pm, Monday to Saturday. Also open on Sundays during the summer months. Open all year. Tel: 01974 298415.

The sign at the Tregaron Kite Centre

On the walk you will pass the Tregaron Kite Centre, which is not only a museum and information centre but has on offer tea, coffee and delicious home-made Welsh cakes. The centre, run by volunteers, was once a church school. Here you can learn about the local history as well as the red kite. Do not miss the superb Cors Caron Mural which was designed and made by eighty local children, aged 8 to 11 years, from materials in the environment such as peat, heather, berries, reeds, sheep's wool and feathers. Open 10.30am to 4.30pm from Easter to the end of September. Also open 12noon to 4.00pm on Saturdays and Sundays in the winter.

The Walk

1. From the car park, go left to the square. Just before reaching the Talbot Hotel, go left to pass the building on your right and walk ahead to a kissing gate. Cross a stile on the right and follow an enclosed track for about 50 metres to a stile on the left.

2. Slant left uphill to pass a telegraph pole and then go downhill to a dip where there is a kissing gate. Walk gradually uphill to a stile at the far end of the upper line of trees. Slant slightly right uphill to the next stile. Go left through a field gate then cross this field diagonally, uphill at first but, further on, descend to a stile in the far right corner. Walk ahead with a fence and lane on the left until you reach a stile.

3. Turn right along the lane and ignore a bridleway on the right to

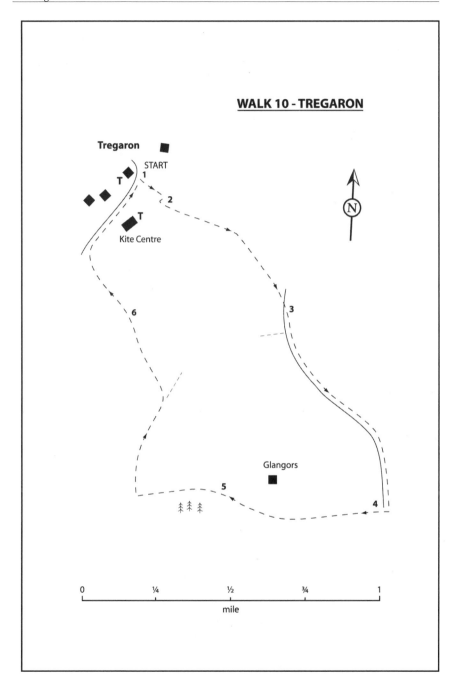

WALK 10 - TREGARON

Tregaron

START

T 1

T

Kite Centre

2

6

3

Glangors

5

4

0 ¼ ½ ¾ 1

mile

Pencefn Drysgol. Continue along the lane, which soon goes uphill. Look back for views to Cors Caron. The lane levels and becomes bordered by trees and, further on, descends to cross a stream. In about another 300 metres, turn right along the access track for Glangors.

4. In about 300 metres, there is a gate across the track. Do not go through it, but go left on a path to have a fence and some trees on your right. Keep ahead between fences. This section can be rather wet. The path bends to the right and continues beside a wall. Ignore a track coming from Glangors and walk on until you arrive at a field gate.

5. With a fence on the left, follow a track through the field and over a rise. Walk downhill to another gate. With a plantation on the left, head downhill, slightly right, to join a surfaced track coming from a house on the left. Turn right along it, through open land. Go through a small gate at a cattle grid and, in about another 400 metres, cross a stile on the left. Slant right downhill through the field to a stile in the far right bottom corner. Go slightly right over a stream and cross the side of the hill to a stile above trees. From here are views of Tregaron and Cors Caron.

    The extensive great bog of Cors Caron forms a 2000 acre National Nature Reserve through which flows the River Teifi. Public access is from a car park on the B4343 about three miles north of Tregaron. The bog is rich in sphagnum mosses and plants such as cotton grass, bog asphodel and sundew. Many wetland birds, including moorhen, snipe and water rail are present but not easily seen. Whooper swans visit in winter.

6. Walk half-right downhill to the right hand corner of the field. Cross a stile at a gate and go left for a few metres to another stile. Slant right through the field to pass under wires and go through a dip to join another path which comes in from the left. Cross a stile in the far corner of the field and follow the left-hand fence to a kissing gate. Turn right along the lane and in about 200 metres you will see The Kite Centre on your right. Continue along the lane to the Square and the Rhiannon Celtic Design Centre and Tearoom.

11. Lampeter

Route: A very pleasant walk along woodland tracks and hillside paths. Some climbing, mainly at the beginning of the walk.

Distance: 5 miles.

How to get there: Lampeter is on the A485, south of Aberystwyth.

Public Transport: Buses from Aberystwyth, Aberaeron and Carmarthen.

Start: The crossroads and fountain in the main street at the meeting point of the A475 with the A485.

Map: Explorer 199.

In the 18th century, the small market town of Lampeter in the Teifi Valley was an important droving centre, where cattle and sheep were gathered before making the long journey to markets in England. Nowadays, Lampeter is known mainly for its university college, St David's, the oldest in Wales. It was founded in 1822 to provide higher education for young men training for the Anglican ministry. Women are now admitted as students and the college became integrated with the University of Wales in 1971. The founder was an Englishman Thomas Burgess, Bishop of St David's, and the original buildings were based on the layout and design of the Oxford colleges. The site was donated by the Harford family and they also gave the fountain in Harford Square. On the college site is a large earth mound, the remains of a Norman Castle. It was attacked in the 12th century by Owain Gwynedd and, about two hundred years later, by Owain Glyndwr.

The Tea Shop

Et Voilá, with its small courtyard, is at the back of Caxton News near Harford Square. Baguettes are one of the specialities and a huge choice of fillings is on offer. There is also a good selection of delicious cakes and pastries. Open from 9.00am to 5.00pm. Closed on Sundays.

The Walk

1. From the fountain, take the A485 in the direction of Tregaron. Pass the university entrance on the right and go directly over a crossroads. After passing a rugby field, turn right along a lane.

2. Pass the Rugby Clubhouse on your right and go through a gate beside a cattle grid. Cross a bridge over the River Dulas and follow a track uphill through the field towards Mount Pleasant Farm. When the track goes right to the farm, keep ahead to pass buildings on the right. Walk uphill to a small gate and follow a clear path along the edge of the trees. Pass through a gate into a wood. On reaching a stile beside a gate entering a field, do not cross, but take a stile on your left into more woodland.

3. Follow the track as it veers left before circling right to have a valley below on the left. On reaching a gate at the edge of the forest, continue ahead on a green track. Go through another track into woodlands. In about 600 metres, you will pass a former quarry on the right. In another 800 metres, at a fork, ignore a path on the left, and the track ahead. Bear right on another track and walk uphill.

4. Follow the track to a turning point and continue ahead on a narrower track. In about another 200 metres, the track/path makes a definite right bend (this is before it goes downhill). Here, go left on a lesser path. In a few metres, cross a slighter path and climb a stile at the edge of the wood. Turn right and, shortly, pass a hill fort on your left.

    The Iron Age hill fort of Castell Allt Goch was one of several defended Celtic homesteads in the area. It was protected by a ditch with a wooden palisade. On your way to this point, you may have noticed a conspicuous tower on a hill to the north. This is the 126ft Derry Ormond Tower, which was built in 1826 by John Jones of Derry Ormond House. It has 365 steps.

5. At a point where there is a fence in front of you, go left uphill almost to the level of the hill fort, then go downhill to a stile on the right. Cross the stile and follow a green track bordered by gorse. Climb a stile at a gate to have a wood on the right and walk on through the fields. Descend to the stile at the edge of the woodlands seen earlier on the walk – and retrace your steps to the start and Et Voila.

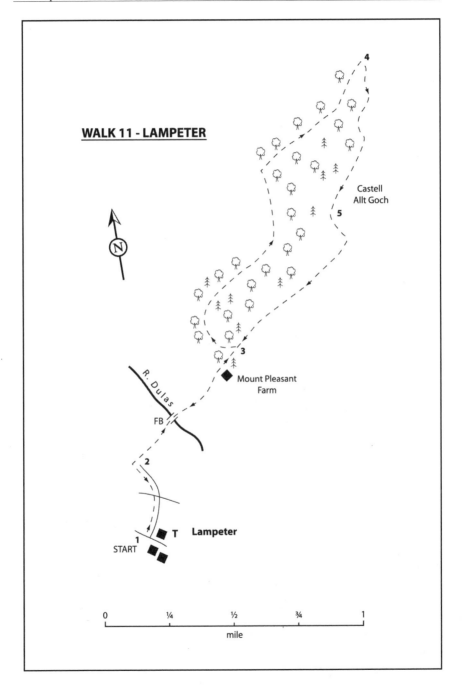

WALK 11 - LAMPETER

Castell
Allt Goch

R. Dulas

FB

Mount Pleasant
Farm

T   **Lampeter**

START

0   ¼   ½   ¾   1

mile

12. Aberporth

Route: A lovely, varied walk following a cliff path to Tresaith and a return through fields with views of the coast. Some road walking.

Distance: 4½ miles.

How to get there: Aberporth is on the B4333, off the A487 and north-east of Cardigan.

Public Transport: Buses from Cardigan and Aberystwyth (change at Cross Inn).

Start: Car park above the beach.

Map: Explorer 198.

The small seaside resort of Aberporth began as a few mud cottages on a spur between the two present beaches. Known as Pen Trwyn Cynwyl, the spur is named after a Celtic missionary. It is believed he visited the area in the 6th century and the parish church is named after him. By the 18th century, the village had developed a maritime trade and several local families owned sailing vessels. Aberporth became famous for its herring shoals and, for a while, was one of the most important fishing ports in Wales. Large numbers of herring, which fed and spawned in the bay, were caught in nets cast from rocks and rowing boats. After being salted, the herring were stored in layers for the winter in a room or shed that each family kept for this purpose. Because of dwindling catches, herring fishing declined in the early 20th century. Holiday makers started to arrive in Aberporth at the end of the 19th century. Today, the bay remains a very pleasant spot with shallow waters, two sandy beaches, and rock pools at low tide.

The Tea Shop

Located close to the beach, the Beach Café serves a wide range of refreshments from breakfasts, morning coffee, snacks and meals to ice cream and cold drinks. Afternoon teas are available with a choice of sandwiches, bara brith and scones with jam and cream. Open daily, 9.30am to late afternoon, or 6.00 – 7.00pm (according to season) from Easter to late September.

Tresaith Beach, Aberporth

The Walk

1. From the car park, walk around the cove and, after crossing a bridge, go left on the slipway. Follow a path above the top of the beach and, about half-way along it, turn right on a stepped path. Follow it uphill through the trees and emerge near a children's playground. Go left to a road and turn left downhill. Pass the Headland Hotel on the right and immediately bear right. At the end of the lane, walk ahead on the path and go left at a corner. In a few paces you will emerge on the cliff path.

2. Turn right to have fine views of the coastline. Continue along the path and pass a caravan site. Cross a track to a stile and, in about another 500 metres, descend a path to the beach and road at Tresaith.

   Tresaith is an abbreviation of Traeth Saith – the beach of seven – and, according to legend, the name is derived from the seven Irish princesses who landed on the beach after being cast adrift by their father in a boat without oars or sails. They settled nearby and married the wealthiest farmers in the area.

   The Afon Saith once flowed into the bay but during the last Ice Age, the valley was blocked by a glacier and the melt water cut a channel further east. After the ice melted, boulder clay prevented the stream from resuming its old course and Afon Saith, since then, has cascaded over cliffs in a waterfall on the east side of the bay. In the 19th century, sailing boats landed at Tresaith. They brought in limestone and anthracite for the two lime kilns near the beach, which provided local farmers with lime as fertiliser. If the tide is out, it is possible to walk along the shore to the beach at Penbryn.

3. After exploring the beach, follow the road uphill. On reaching a road junction, ignore a road on the right and walk uphill to a fork. Turn right and follow the lane over a stream. In a few metres, cross a stile on the right and walk along the left side of the field to another stile.

4. Follow a track across a stream and bear right through woodland. In 50 metres, go left around a sharp bend to pass above the route just walked. In about 100 metres, bear right on a clear path. It

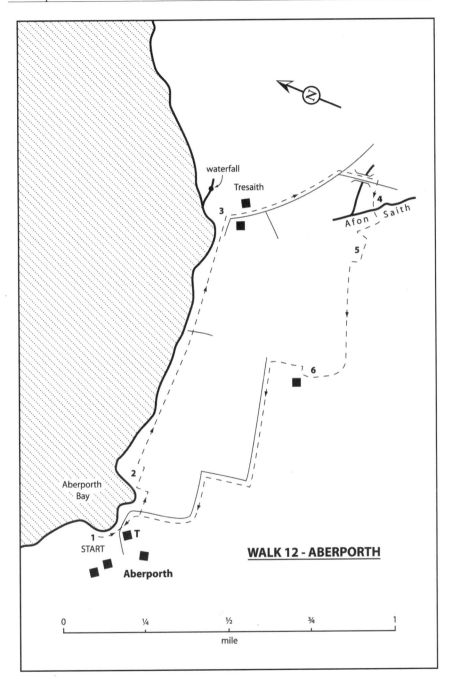

waterfall

Tresaith

3

Aberporth
Bay

2

1

T

START

Aberporth

Afon Saith

4

5

6

WALK 12 - ABERPORTH

0   ¼   ½   ¾   1

mile

bends to the left to have a rough field on the right. On joining another path, continue ahead to a gate and track.

5. Turn left for a few paces then go right uphill along a track. In about 25 metres go left at a waymarked post. Follow the path to a stile and field. Walk along the right boundary but, in about 50 metres, join a track at the edge of the field and keep ahead. Go through the right-hand gate ahead and walk along the left boundary of fields until you emerge in a large field. Walk through the middle of this field to a stile but do not cross it. Bear right along the left side of the field to a gate.

6. Walk downhill along the track in the direction of the sea. The track bends right and left to reach farm buildings. Veer right with the track downhill and emerge on a lane. Turn left to cross-roads and bear right. In 300 metres go left with the road downhill to the Beach Café and car park.

13. Penbryn

Route: After visiting an ancient church, the route follows quiet lanes before returning along a scenic stretch of coastal path.

Distance: 4 miles.

How to get there: Penbryn can be reached by minor roads off the A487.

Public Transport: Infrequent buses from Cardigan.

Start: Llanborth car park near the café at Penbryn.

Map: Explorer 198.

The ancient settlement of Penbryn lies in the wooded valley of the Hoffnant, just a few hundred metres inland from Cardigan Bay. It is now owned by the National Trust. The lane or a woodland path may be followed to the sands of Traeth Penbryn from where, at low tide, the beach extends westwards to Tresaith. In the past, smugglers used the beach and valley for their illicit trading. The sandy shore is the habitat of the sand eel and it may be found in the shallows or just below the sand at low water. They were dug up for use as human food in times gone by.

The Tea Shop

Close to the Llanborth car park, you will find Penbryn Café, which offers light lunches, snacks and home baking. The menu includes jacket potatoes, toasties, sandwiches, Welsh cakes, flapjacks and a variety of hot and cold drinks. Seating is inside the café or outside at picnic tables. Open at weekends from Easter until late May then everyday until the end of September. Hours at the beginning and end of the season are 11.00am to 4.30pm. Opening hours are longer in the height of the season. The café is also open two evenings a week for home-cooked dinner. Farmhouse accommodation and a small number of caravans are available for those who wish to stay awhile in this idyllic spot. Tel:01239 810389.

The Walk

1. From the back of the car park, take a stepped path downhill

through woodland to cross a footbridge. Follow the path as it bears right and rises to a wall. Turn right and ignore a path on the right. In a few metres, at another junction, bear left and go through a kissing gate. With trees on your left, walk uphill to a gate and turn right along the lane to St Michael's Church.

> The ancient church of St Michael is thought to be one of the oldest churches in Wales. Parts are 12th century and the building contains a Norman font and a 'weeping chancel'. The churchyard is circular and it is believed to be a pre-Christian religious site. A timber church may have stood here before the stone structure and, according to legend, it was to be replaced by a permanent church on another site. Its stonework, built during the day, was taken each night to Penbryn by mysterious forces. Eventually, the new site was abandoned and the stone church was built at Penbryn. In the churchyard is the grave of Mrs Anne Adeliza Puddiecombe, a romantic novelist, who wrote under the name of Allen Raine. She lived in Tresaith at the beginning of the 20th century. Her extremely popular novels include the titles 'A Welsh Witch' and 'Queen of the Rushes'.

2. After visiting the church, retrace your steps along the lane. Do not return through the gate but continue walking along the lane. Ignore the lane on the left to Penbryn and walk uphill to a junction. Turn left and, at a left bend, ignore a lane on the right for Sarnau. Cross a bridge over the Hoffnant and ignore the next lane on the right.

3. Pass Penmorfa Chapel on the left and turn left at the next junction. Ignore a track on the left with a Private Road notice. When the lane bends sharp right, go left on a dead end lane. Pass Morfa Ganol and some farm buildings and, in about 50 metres, turn right through a gate at a footpath signpost.

4. Walk ahead on an enclosed track. On reaching a gate into a field, cross a stile to the right of it and follow a path between the fence and hedge around two sides of the field. In 300 metres, ignore a stile on the right and bear left along the coastal path.

5. In a few metres, there are views of an island below. The path

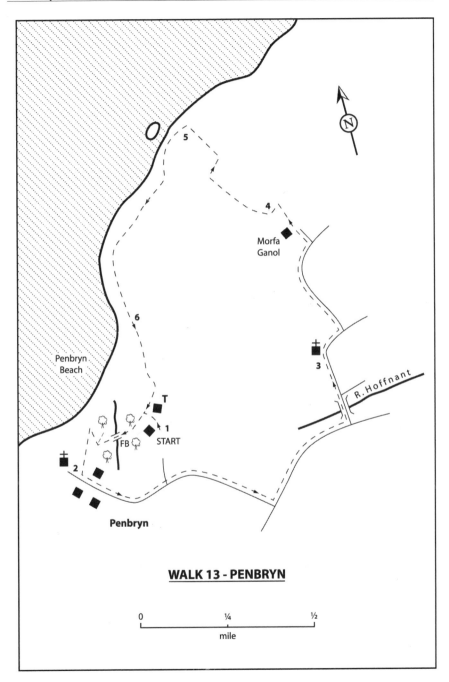

Penbryn Beach

Morfa Ganol

R. Hoffnant

Penbryn

FB

START

T

WALK 13 - PENBRYN

0   ¼   ½

mile

makes a steep descent to a stile and crosses a stream. Ignore a path going inland on the left and continue along the coast. After rising to a stile, walk on uphill to the right-hand corner of a fence. Bear right beside it to a stile. Walk along the edge of a field to a stile in the corner and follow a path to a kissing gate.

6. Turn right along a track. In about 100 metres, you will have views of Penbryn Beach. On reaching a footpath signpost, bear right with the track downhill. At buildings, go through the gate ahead and turn left to Penbryn Café and the car park.

Coastal scenery near Penbryn

14. Llangranog

Route: A superb, varied walk taking in spectacular cliff scenery and attractive woodlands.

Distance: 4 miles.

How to get there: Llangranog is on the B4321, off the A487, and south-west of Newquay.

Public Transport: Infrequent buses from Cardigan.

Start: Car park near the beach at Llangranog.

Map: Explorer 198.

The picturesque seaside village of Llangranog lies in a steep valley which opens out onto a sandy beach. A church was founded here in the early 6th century by St Carantoc, a Celtic saint. According to legend, he was whittling a staff outside his cave one day, when a pigeon flew off with a piece of the bark. Believing this to be a

Llangranog from the cliffs

message from God, he followed the pigeon through the valley and built a church on the spot where the bird eventually laid the bark. This is near the site of the present church. The settlement grew and the community engaged in farming and fishing. Being in a sheltered position between high cliffs, the cove at Llangranog became a port in the 18th century and household goods, salt and limestone were imported. Wooden coasting vessels were built in the shipyards near the foreshore. On the beach is a prominent rock known as Carreg Bica, the Devil's Tooth, to which is attached a legend. A long time ago, the Devil, whilst suffering raging toothache, wrenched out the offending fang and hurled it to this beach.

The Tea Shop

The popular Patio Tearoom and Restaurant is situated directly above the beach at Llangranog. The varied menu includes main meals, soups, baguettes, and a choice of delicious cakes including scones and cream. Open from 11.00am to 6.00pm every day from Easter to late October. At other times, open at weekends only.

The Walk

1. Walk onto the beach and climb the steps to the left of the Patio Tearoom. The path winds uphill along the edge of the cliffs and continues above coves to give fine views of the coastline. Have a fence and field on your right and go uphill to a small gate. Turn left along a track. On reaching a bench, you may like to take a diversion onto the Lochtyn promontory. The cliffs here are eroded underneath and it is dangerous to stand close to the edge.

    The Lochtyn peninsula consists of the hill, Pen y Badell, the promontory and the small island at its end, Ynys Lochtyn. On the summit of the hill is Pendinas Lochtyn, an Iron Age hill fort. Look out for rock pipit, chough, raven and the occasional peregrine. Grey seals, bottle-nosed dolphins and porpoise are often spotted offshore along this part of the Cardigan coast.

2. Return to the main path and continue uphill along it. At a fork, go left to take a less distinct path. It levels, then rises and becomes quite steep to give extensive views. On reaching a track, go left but, when it rises to a field gate, go left to a stile.

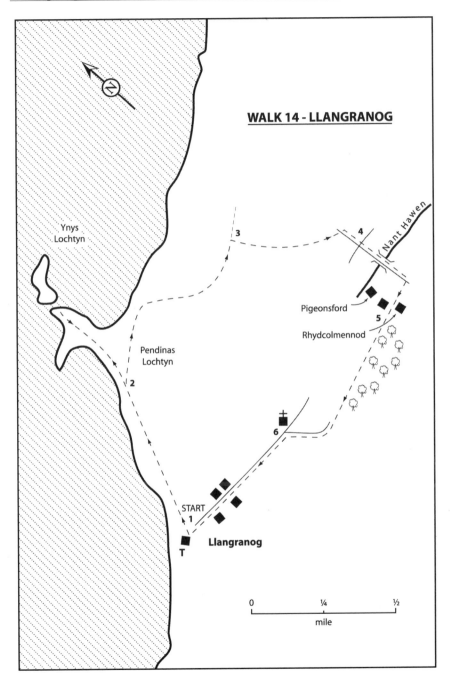

WALK 14 - LLANGRANOG

Ynys
Lochtyn

Nant Hawen

3

4

Pigeonsford

5

Rhydcolmennod

Pendinas
Lochtyn

2

6

START
1

Llangranog

T

0   ¼   ½

mile

Descend above cliffs to a stile and immediately turn right through a kissing gate.

3. Follow a fence on the right to another kissing gate then slant left across the field to a kissing gate in a corner. Continue beside the left boundary of two fields to a track and follow it to a lane. Turn right and cross directly over a road.

4. Cross a bridge over Nant Hawen and walk uphill to pass the entrance to The Walled Garden of Pigeonsford on your right. In about another 100 metres, turn right along the drive to Rhydcolmennod. Pass the house on your right and go through a gate to have a building on your left. Cross a stile and follow a path beside the garden.

5. Walk towards woodlands but do not go through the old gate-posts. Have an old wall on your left and follow the path through trees to a small gate. Continue above a valley and ignore a path on the left. Emerge on a road and turn right to a junction. On your right is the church of St Carnog.

St Carnog's Church was rebuilt in 1884 but still contains some earlier features including a Norman font. In the church-yard is a grave to Sarah Rees, a 19th-century master mariner who was known as Cranogwen.

6. Turn left along the road and follow it to the tearoom and car park.

15. New Quay

Route: A fairly energetic coastal walk offering superb views but with some steep sections. The route returns along a pleasant valley, tracks and lanes.

Distance: 6 miles.

How to get there: New Quay is on the A486, south-west of Aberystwyth.

Public Transport: Buses from Aberystwyth and Cardigan (change at Cross Inn).

Start: New Quay harbour.

Map: Explorer 198.

New Quay has grown from a small fishing hamlet in the 18th century to the present-day, busy holiday resort. During the shipbuilding boom of the 19th century, New Quay, with its safe anchorage,

The harbour

became one of the main centres and hundreds of skilled workmen were employed in the shipyards. Small sloops, schooners and larger ships for sailing to the Americas and Australia were built on the local beaches. The main harbour pier was built in 1835 with stone quarried from the cliffs above Parson's cave. New Quay was also notorious for its smugglers and the headland was said to be riddled with caves containing contraband such as tobacco and brandy brought in from France. The shipping trade declined with the development of the railways and road transport but by then holidaymakers were visiting the area. Dylan Thomas came here in the 1940s and New Quay – along with Laugharne in Carmarthenshire – claims to be the original Llareggub (spell it backwards) in 'Under Milk Wood'. New Quay is now a popular yachting centre.

The Tea Shop

The Old Watch House is now a restaurant overlooking the quay. Main meals and afternoon teas are available and the menu includes baked potatoes, toasted sandwiches, cakes and scones with cream. Open 10.00am to 5.00pm (and some evenings) daily from March to mid October. Tel: 01545 560852.

The Walk

1. At the harbour, face the sea and turn left to pass the Old Watch House and the Tourist Information Centre. Immediately after passing a car park on the left, go left up a road. Cross the first road on the right to take a path between buildings and emerge on the upper terrace. Turn right for about 200 metres then take the cliff path beside a garden. The path makes a long climb above a quarry and passes a stone wall. Continue between gorse to a National Trust sign at a small quarry.

    Birds Rock is one of the most important seabird colonies in Wales. Three to four thousand guillemots nest on the ledges here between March and July along with kittiwakes, fulmars and razorbills. Seals may be spotted, basking on the rocks. Look out for bottle-nosed dolphins and porpoise.

2. Here, you have the choice of an exposed cliff path or a safer path. In a few metres, the paths merge and lead to the old coastguard

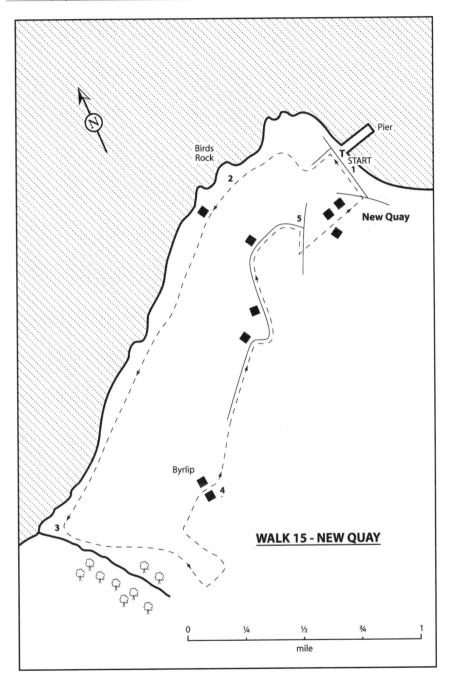

Pier

Birds
Rock

T
START
1

2

5

New Quay

Byrlip

4

3

WALK 15 - NEW QUAY

0   ¼   ½   ¾   1

mile

lookout. Ignore a kissing gate on the left and follow the coastal path to a stile and field. Walk on beside the hedge to the next stile. Shortly, cross a stile at a gate and go downhill beside a fence to the next stile. Descend a steep path to a footbridge and go up steps then through a gate to continue beside a fence. The path passes through a gap and goes downhill between hedges before rising to a stile and field. Continue alongside the right-hand boundary and, in a few metres, go right through a gap. Bear left downhill to a stile and footbridge. Go up to a kissing gate and continue beside a left-hand fence. After going through another kissing-gate, walk downhill to a viewpoint above a small cove.

3. Leave the coast and follow a path inland above a valley. On reaching a path where there is a footbridge on the right and near a National Trust sign, go left to have the stream on your right. At a path junction in 100 metres, turn left on a wide path. Go steadily uphill and, after passing through a small gate, follow the path as it bears right. Pass a garden and shortly bear right between houses to a track.

4. Walk on uphill along the track. Further on, it curves to the left and becomes fairly level as it passes between fields. After a short descent, the track becomes surfaced. Walk on and pass Coybel Lodge and Ty Rhos. After passing a farm, the lane goes downhill to emerge on the A486.

5. Turn right for about 80 metres then go left on a track. In 100 metres, at a fork, go left to pass a house on the right. Continue across grass and go through a gate onto an enclosed track. At its end, go through a kissing gate and bear right on a lane. Pass a car park and cross over the main road to another road and follow it downhill to New Quay harbour and The Old Watch House.

16. Aberaeron

Route: A fairly easy walk following riverside, woodland and field paths to Llanerchaeron and a return along the old railway trackbed.

Distance: 6 miles.

How to get there: Aberaeron is on the A487, south-west of Aberystwyth.

Public Transport: Buses from Aberystwyth, Cardigan and Carmarthen.

Start: The Tourist Information Centre near the harbour.

Map: Explorer 198.

Aberaeron was a small fishing hamlet until the early 19th century when Alban Thomas Jones and his wife were bequeathed a fortune by Lewis Gwynne of Mynachdy on condition they adopted the surname Gwynne. Reverend Alban Gwynne then decided to develop the harbour, and in 1807 obtained parliamentary permission to build piers and a harbour at the mouth of the River Aeron.

Aberaeron harbour

The harbour was completed in 1811 and Aberaeron grew into a busy little port exporting butter, cattle and wool, and importing coal and groceries. Several boats were engaged in the herring industry and on the southern side of the harbour were shipbuilders' yards. Elegant houses were built for the shipowners and merchants. Aberaeron, with its carefully laid out streets, squares and Georgian to early Victorian houses, is a fine example of early 19th-century town planning. John Nash is reputed to have drawn a plan for the town but most of the building took place after his death in 1835. The shipping trade declined with the coming of the railways but the picturesque little town continued to thrive as a holiday resort.

The Tea Shop

The Hive on the Quay is renowned for its honey ice cream and superb home-made food made from local organic produce. Specialities include fresh seafood dishes, unusual salads and a fine selection of cakes, including honey cake. Sandwiches, ice cream sundaes and scones with cream are also on offer. The restaurant has lots of greenery and there is a conservatory. Open 10.30am to 5.00pm from Easter to November. Open later in August. Check opening times if visiting at the beginning or near the end of the season. Tel: 01545 570445.

The Walk

1. Leave the Tourist Information Centre by having the harbour on your right and pass The Hive on the Quay. Cross a wooden footbridge and go left to the road. Cross and bear left a few paces then turn right to have the river on your left. Pass through woodlands and ignore a footbridge and paths leading off. On reaching a road, cross with care and turn left over the bridge.

2. When the road bends left, go right along a lane called Bro Allt-y-Graig. Ignore a road on the left and keep ahead. Walk downhill and, at a slight right bend, go ahead on a track into woodland. From a gate, continue along the lower path and, after passing an old quarry on the left, descend a path to the lane. Turn left and, after passing a farm on the right, continue ahead on a track that goes gently downhill. Ignore a stile on the right and cross the stile ahead. Follow a track to a field.

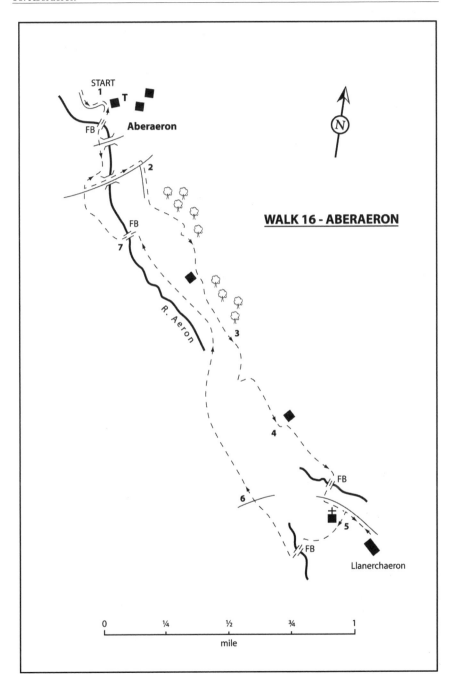

START
1
T
Aberaeron
FB
2
FB
7
R. Aeron
3
4
FB
6
5
FB
Llanerchaeron

WALK 16 - ABERAERON

N

0   ¼   ½   ¾   1
mile

3. Immediately, leave the field by going right on a path that swings left to pass below the field. Continue along this path and, further on, keep a fence on your right. Pass ruins on your left and cross a stile. After crossing another stile, bear right into a field then slant left to follow the left-hand boundary to a gate opening. Continue along the left side of a field to a stile and farm access track.

4. Turn left and, in about 20 metres, go right to cross a stile beside a gate. Walk on into woodland and, after crossing a stile, pass a ruin on the left. Continue along a track for about 50 metres, then go left uphill to a stile. Go downhill through woodland and cross a footbridge over the River Aeron. Walk straight across the middle of the field to a gate and turn left. Pass a church on your right and walk on another 200 metres to a footpath on the right. If you wish to visit Llanerchaeron, follow the lane for about another 150 metres to the entrance gates.

Llanerchaeron has survived almost unchanged since the 18th century, when there were many, small self-sufficient Welsh gentry estates. The house was designed in the 1790s by John Nash for William Lewis, and the estate stayed in the same family until bequeathed to the National Trust in 1989. It is a rare survivor as most estates have vanished or been split up. Apart from the house, there is a brewery, laundry, dairy and servants' quarters. The home farm buildings included cowsheds, barns, a granary and stables. There are plans to restore a lake in the grounds and the carriage drive around it, where Mary Ashby Lewis, who married Colonel Lewis's son John, used to enjoy drives in her dog cart. After her husband died, she ran the estate for the next 62 years until she died at the age of 104. Her nephew, Thomas Powell Lewes, inherited the estate and he modernised it by introducing electricity, but otherwise continued with the old traditions. It was his son, John Powell Ponsonby Lewes, who bequeathed the estate to the National Trust.

The estate is being restored into a working organic farm. Organic fruit and vegetables are produced in the walled gardens. Following restoration, the National Trust opened the house and gardens to the public in June 2002. Opening hours are 11.00am to 5.00pm (closed Mondays and Tuesdays) from late March to early November.

5. Return to the footpath and pass through a kissing gate into a field. Go ahead, slightly left, across the large field and pass the corner of woodlands on your right. Go through a small gate and cross a footbridge. On reaching an access track to a house on your right, go left for about 30 metres, then right on a track. Follow it to a lane and cross directly to a track.

    This is the trackbed of the railway branch line that linked Lampeter with Aberaeron. There were several halts including Llanerchaeron. Completed in 1911, the line closed to passengers forty years later, but milk trains between Lampeter and the creamery at Felin Fach continued until 1973.

6. Continue ahead and when the main track bends right, go through the gate ahead to continue along a narrow fenced track between fields. Further on, the track passes close to the river, and through woodlands. Eventually, you will pass a house on the right and some picnic tables on the left. Walk on along the track for about another 80 metres, then go left to cross a footbridge over the river.

7. Follow a path between fields and, at a junction go right to have a wall on the left. Cross a drive then take a path to a stile and field. Walk on beside the left-hand boundary to a stile at a gate. Continue along a road and, on reaching the A482, cross with care and turn right along the pavement. In about 100 metres, go left to retrace your steps beside the river to the start.

17. Devil's Bridge

Route: A downhill walk through woodlands to the River Rheidol is followed by a steady climb out of the valley. There are superb views throughout the walk.

Distance: 4½ miles.

How to get there: Devil's Bridge is on the A4120 east of Aberystwyth. The A4120 leaves the A44 at Ponterwyd. From Tregaron take the B4343 north to Devil's Bridge.

Public Transport: The Vale of Rheidol narrow gauge railway line links Aberystwyth with Devil's Bridge. Trains run daily from Easter to late October except on Fridays and Sundays at the beginning and end of the season.

Start: Vale of Rheidol Railway Station, Devil's Bridge (or the car park opposite the station).

Map: Explorer 213.

Devil's Bridge takes its name from a medieval bridge that spans the River Mynach. According to a local legend, the Devil, knowing that a structure was needed, built the bridge with the intention of claiming the soul of the first living thing to cross it. An old woman, who wanted to cross the river to retrieve her stray cow, outwitted the Devil by tossing a piece of bread across the bridge for a dog to chase. The Devil had to make do with the soul of the dog while the old woman safely drove her cow back across the bridge. It is thought that the monks of Strata Florida probably built it to gain access to sheep pasture on the opposite side of the river. In the 18th century, another wider bridge was constructed above it, and in the early 20th century a third, modern iron bridge was built directly above it.

During the 16th century the gorge was the haunt of a notorious gang of robbers and murderers, two brothers and a sister, known as plant de bat (bat children). They lived in a cave below the gorge but were eventually smoked out and hanged at Rhayader. To view the bridges and a spectacular series of waterfalls, there is an admission charge.

Devil's Bridge is the terminus of the Vale of Rheidol Railway, which was originally constructed to carry ore from the lead mines in Cwm Rheidol to Aberystwyth. Construction started in 1901 and by the end of 1902 both freight and passenger trains operated on the line. From the 1930s, the trains mainly carried tourists as the lead mines had closed and local people preferred the new bus service. It was the last steam train to be run by British Rail but it was eventually taken over by the Brecon Mountain Railway in 1989. Because of fire risk – the line runs mainly through woodland – only oil burning locomotives are now used. The train rises over 600ft on its journey from Aberystwyth and the views over the valley are magnificent. Oak and coniferous woodlands cover the steep valley sides of Cwm Rheidol, part of which is a national nature reserve. The oak woods were heavily cropped about the time of the 1914 to 1918 war for use in the South Wales coalmines. Lead mining took place in the valley during the early years of the 20th century and the ore was carried to the railway by an aerial ropeway. Amongst the sessile oak woods are an abundance of lichens, liverworts, mosses and ferns. Look out for pied flycatcher, wood warbler and redstart.

The Tea Shop

If you have made your journey to Devil's Bridge by the scenic Vale of Rheidol Railway, the Station Café is the ideal place for refreshments at the end of your walk. Snacks on offer include fresh and toasted sandwiches, rolls, muffins, Welsh cakes and scones with cream. Coffee, tea and cold drinks are available. Days and hours of opening fit in with the trains. Tel: 01970 625819 (train times).

The Walk

1.   Starting from the Vale of Rheidol Railway Station, walk out to the road and turn right. Ignore a road on the left to Tregaron and follow the road uphill for another 200 metres then turn right through a field gate. Pass a garden on the right and walk ahead to pass trees on the left. Walk downhill and ignore paths leading off. A few metres before reaching trees at the end of the field, go left and walk through a small patch of grassland to more trees. The path descends along the top edge of woodlands. The Vale of Rheidol railway line can be seen below on your right. Ignore a descending path but, in about another 60 metres, take a clear path on the right. It descends to a small gate.

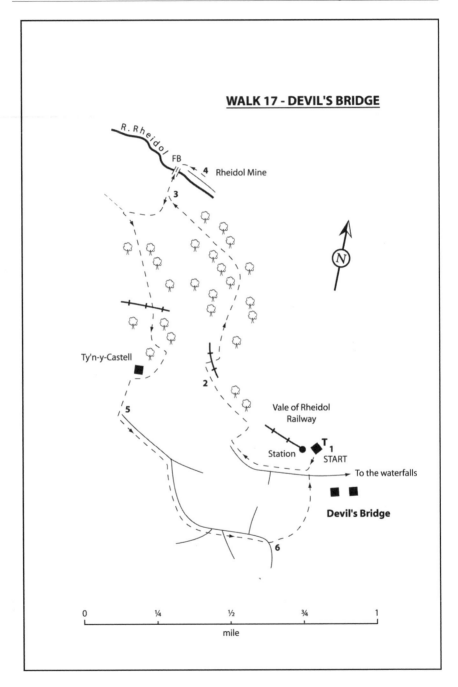

WALK 17 - DEVIL'S BRIDGE

2. Follow the right-hand fence to a stile, then go left alongside the railway for a few metres before crossing the track to a path on the right. In about another 100 metres, cross a stile on the left. Bear right beside the railway line and cross a stile on the left. Follow the fence on your right to a small gate and cross the line to another gate. Follow a path that soon bears right, then left, downhill. On joining a track, turn left. Pass through an area of scattered trees to reach a gate. The route turns left here but you may like to make a diversion to the river before continuing on the walk.

3. Descend to a footbridge and turn right for about 100 metres or so to a plaque giving information about the nearby Rheidol lead and zinc mine.

4. Retrace your steps uphill through the gate and continue on a path, uphill. Follow a fence on your right for about 200 metres. Pass a gate on your right and, in a few more paces, go left uphill on a grassy path. From the top edge of the wood there is a good view of the valley and mine. Go through the gate and cross the railway track to another. Continue uphill on a clear path through the woods until you almost reach a field. Follow a track to the left and right along the edge of fields and pass in front of Ty'n-y-Castell. Follow the access track to the road and turn left.

5. Walk downhill and, when the lane bends left, go ahead on a lane. It bends left to give wide views over the surrounding countryside. Join another road at a junction and turn left. Ignore a lane on the right and keep left to a road. Turn right for 50 metres and, when the lane bends right, keep ahead on a track between a bungalow and a house.

6. Go through a gate and follow the track, which soon bends to the left. Before reaching trees, go left to pass them on your right. Further downhill, have a fence on your right. Cross a stile on your right and follow a track to the road, station and café.

18. Aberystwyth

Route: A gentle climb to the summit of Pendinas is rewarded by superb views of the surrounding countryside and Cardigan Bay.

Distance: 4 miles.

How to get there: Aberystwyth is on the A44, west of Newtown.

Public Transport: Trains from Birmingham and Shrewsbury to Aberystwyth. Buses from Machynlleth, Cardigan and other nearby towns.

Start: Aberystwyth pier.

Map: Explorer 213.

The town of Aberystwyth can be traced back to the 13th century when Edward I built his castle here. However, the town's name is derived from an earlier Norman fortification, built in the 11th century, a little further south on the River Ystwyth. Aberystwyth became an important herring port and the fish was preserved with salt or by smoking before being supplied to markets throughout Britain. In the 17th and 18th centuries, hundreds of ships were built in the

Constitution Hill from the sea front

shipyards around the harbour. This activity declined on the arrival of the railway in the 1860s, but the town expanded rapidly to accommodate the Victorian visitors. Thomas Savin, a railway businessman, built a fantastic, mammoth hotel near the pier to accommodate the influx of holidaymakers, but his speculation failed and he became bankrupt. A voluntary committee, intent on establishing a non-denominational Welsh university, bought the neo-Gothic building and established it as a university college. It is still part of the university, but the main campus is on Penglais Hill. On the campus is the National Library of Wales, which contains millions of books, including ancient Welsh manuscripts.

The Tea Shop

The Mecca Coffee House is an atmospheric little coffee house standing opposite the Mecca Tea and Coffee Merchants where you can buy many different varieties of coffee beans and teas. On offer in the coffee house is an excellent choice of speciality teas as well as coffee. The menu includes croissants, sandwiches and a fine selection of cakes and pastries. Open 8.00am until 7.00pm, Mondays to Saturdays.

The Walk

1. With your back to the pier, turn right to have the sea on your right. Pass the old university buildings, the church and the castle ruins.

   Edward I built Aberystwyth Castle during his campaign of castle building to suppress the Welsh. Work started in 1277 and the town was made a free borough the same year, but the castle was not completed until 1289. It was besieged by the Welsh in 1294 but held firm. In 1404 the castle was taken by Owain Glyndwr and held by the Welsh until 1408, when it was recaptured by Prince Henry, the future Henry V. In the early 17th century, Charles I gave permission to Thomas Bushell to establish a mint in the castle. Bushell refined silver from the ore of the nearby lead mines. During the Civil War, the castle was garrisoned for the king, but was taken by parliamentary forces in 1646 and afterwards blown up.

2. Continue beside the sea and, at the end of houses on the left, go left to pass the harbour on your right. Ignore a road on the left and walk on around the harbour. Pass a small car park on the right and, a few paces after passing a brick building on the right, turn left up steps between a wall and building. Bear right to the A487 and turn right to cross the bridge over the River Rheidol.

3. Follow the A487 past the fire station and then turn right along a road. Ignore a road on the left and walk on until a bridge is about 40 metres in front of you. Take an enclosed path on the left to a road. Turn right and in 120 metres go through a kissing gate on the left. Follow a clear path gently uphill and pass through a kissing gate to have views of the coast and River Ystwyth. After following the path for over half a mile, and at a point where it starts to descend steeply, go left on a short path to reach a higher path. Bear left and follow the path uphill to the Wellington monument on Pendinas.

> The cannon barrel shaped monument on the 415 foot summit of Pendinas was erected in 1852 to commemorate the Duke of Wellington's victory at the Battle of Waterloo. The original intention was to build a statue of the Duke on horseback on the top of the column. During the Iron Age, a settlement of about 100 people occupied the summit. The fort, at first, was only on the northern summit – this is on private land but can be viewed from the path. Later, the southern hilltop (on which the monument is built) was enclosed with a bank and ditches, and the total defended area covered over nine acres. In the southern enclosure are several house platforms. Excavations in the 1930s uncovered a Roman coin, beads and Iron Age pottery. The fort was probably occupied for about 400 years, but would have been abandoned after the arrival of the Romans.

4. Leave the monument on a clear path in the general direction of Aberystwyth. Walk downhill to a fence then bear right beside it. Go through a kissing gate and continue on a path to another kissing gate. Cross a track and follow a track for about 100 metres, then go through a kissing gate on the left.

5. The path descends gradually beside and through trees to a gate.

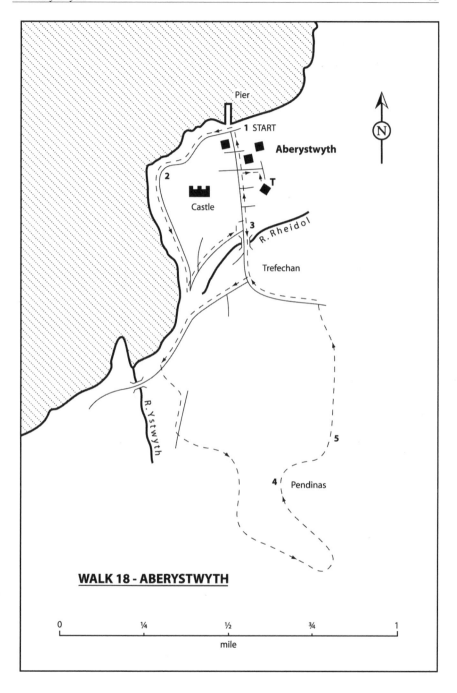

Pier

1 START

Aberystwyth

N

2

T

Castle

3

R. Rheidol

Trefechan

R. Ystwyth

5

4 Pendinas

WALK 18 - ABERYSTWYTH

0   ¼   ½   ¾   1

mile

Walk on between fences to a track near a road, then turn left along the pavement. Go through Trefechan and, after recrossing the road bridge, either go left to retrace your steps to the start or walk ahead up the hill. Continue ahead for the pier but to visit the Mecca Coffee House, turn right along Queen Street. At Chalybeate Street, turn right. The coffee house is on your left.

19. Borth to Aberystwyth

Route: An exhilarating cliff walk with superb coastal views. Some steep paths. Short sections are eroded but these are easy to avoid.

Distance: 5½ miles.

How to get there: Borth is on the B4353, off the A487 and north of Aberystwyth.

Public Transport: Borth and Aberystwyth are on the Shrewsbury to Aberystwyth line. Bus no. 512 (for Ynyslas) from Aberystwyth to Borth (about 1 per hour).

Start: Borth sea front. Finish: Aberystwyth promenade.

Map: Explorer 213.

Borth was a small fishing village until the coming of the railway in 1863 brought visitors to the beach, which stretches over three miles to the Dyfi estuary. The original settlement was Upper Borth on the hillside. During the 19th century, Afon Leri was diverted north from the cliffs and the shingle spit became more stable. Cottages were built along it and, by the time the railway arrived, there was an inn. Coastal defences were built after a great storm in 1877 flooded the road and buildings.

Before the last Ice Age, the coastline was much further west. At very low tides, the tree stumps of a submerged forest are exposed on the beach. During the walk, look out for cormorants drying their wings on the rocks.

The Tea Shop

The Old Summerhouse Tearoom on the summit of Constitution Hill is a popular refreshment stop for walkers. It is run by a community project which supports and helps local people with learning difficulties. On offer are sandwiches, toasties, rolls, soup, snacks, a selection of cakes, and hot and cold drinks. Open 10.00am to 5.00pm daily from Easter to early November.

The Walk

1. In Borth, have the sea on your right and follow the main road –

the B4353 – until it bears left inland. Continue along the road nearest the sea (the B4572) and in about 100 metres go right along a dead end lane to have bungalows on your left and the sea on your right. Follow the road to its end and continue along a path to a small gate. Walk uphill to the memorial, a fine viewpoint.

From the war memorial are wide views of Borth, the bog of Cors Fochno and the Dyfi estuary. A prominent feature in the landscape is the canalised Afon Leri running north in a straight line to the Dyfi estuary. Adjoining the river is the Cors Fochno nature reserve, which is said to be one of the best preserved lowland peat bogs in Britain. Before land was reclaimed for agricultural use in the 19th and early 20th centuries, the bog was much larger than it is now. Local people used to cut peat from the edge of the bog to use as fuel. Since Cors Fochno became a nature reserve, ditches and channels have been dammed to help retain water. Cotton grass, sundew and many varieties of mosses grow in the bog. Birds include curlew, snipe and reed bunting. Otters are present. A public footpath runs along the south side of the reserve, but to visit other parts a permit is necessary. This is obtainable from the Ynyslas Nature Reserve Centre. Cors Fochno and the Ynyslas dunes are part of the Dyfi National Nature Reserve. A variety of plants, including orchids, grow in the dunes, where several kinds of mammals, especially voles and stoats, may be found. The Dyfi estuary is an important feeding ground for wildfowl.

2.   Walk on with a fence on the left and descend to a track near a caravan park. Cross to a footbridge and follow a zigzag path uphill. The path rises above cliffs to a stile then goes downhill before making another steep rise and descent to two footbridges. It rises and falls several times before going downhill to a field. Walk ahead to a footbridge at Wallog.

At Wallog Beach, the remarkable shingle ridge called Sarn Cynfelyn juts out for seven miles into Cardigan Bay. It is believed to be a moraine left from the last Ice Age, but it is also

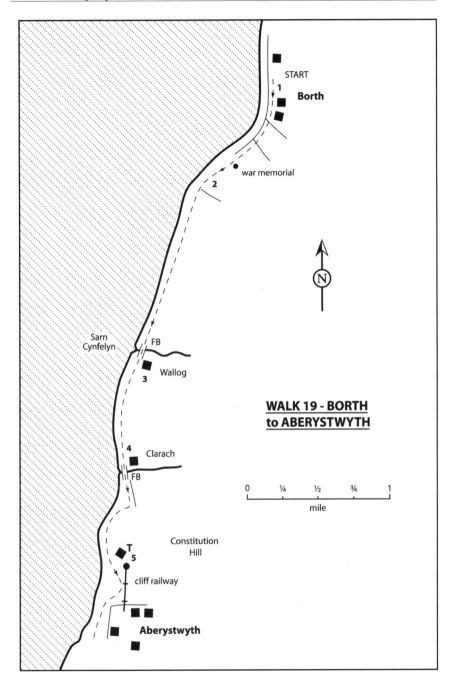

START
Borth

war memorial

Sarn
Cynfelyn   FB
            Wallog

**WALK 19 - BORTH
to ABERYSTWYTH**

Clarach
FB

Constitution
Hill

cliff railway

Aberystwyth

0   ¼   ½   ¾   1
         mile

linked to the legendary flooded fertile plain of Cantre'r
Gwaelod (the Lowland Hundred).

3. Bear right then left to follow the garden wall. A lime kiln can be
    seen near the beach. Walk uphill, taking care to avoid the eroded
    sections. The fence has been moved inland in a few places, and
    there are steps. Continue above the cliffs and follow the path
    downhill to the caravan park at Clarach.

4. Pass the Leisure Centre and a small car park. Cross a footbridge
    over the River Clarach and continue along a road. Follow it as it
    bears left and at the edge of a coniferous wood on your right,
    turn right on a path. Walk uphill beside the trees and, at the end
    of the wood, ignore a stile on the left. Continue along the cliff
    path to the Old Summerhouse Tearooms on Constitution Hill.

    From Constitution Hill are fine views of Aberystwyth and Car-
    digan Bay. Whilst on the 430ft summit, you may like to visit
    the Camera Obscura which was opened in 1985 and is a re-
    construction of a popular Victorian amusement. The lens and
    mirror device produces moving pictures of the surrounding
    area. Constitution Hill has been a popular place to visit since
    1896 when the 778ft long Cliff Railway was built to carry Vic-
    torians to the summit.

5. Follow the main path downhill. It crosses and recrosses the rail-
    way before arriving near Aberystwyth sea front.

20. Machynlleth

Route: A steady climb along moorland tracks and paths offers fine views of the Dyfi valley and the option of a short diversion to a secluded lake.

Distance: 4 miles.

How to get there: Machynlleth is on the A487, north-west of Newtown.

Public Transport: Trains from Shrewsbury, Aberystwyth and Pwllheli. Buses from Dolgellau, Aberystwyth and Newtown.

Start: Car park off Maengwyn Street in the centre of Machynlleth.

Map: Explorer OL23.

Surrounded by hills, Machynlleth is a small, historic town on the south side of Afon Dyfi. In 1291, Edward I granted a charter to hold a market every Wednesday for ever and two fairs a year in Machynlleth to Owain de la Pole, Lord of Powys. Owain Glyndwr was crowned Prince of Wales here in 1404 before envoys from Scotland, Castile and France. He held a parliament in Machynlleth on the site of Parliament House. Dafydd Gam tried to assassinate him whilst he was being crowned, but was captured and imprisoned in Royal House near the clock tower. The impressive memorial clock tower was built in 1874 to celebrate the 21st birthday of Viscount Castlereagh, eldest son of the fifth Marquess of Londonderry. It stands on the site of the Old Town Hall that George Borrow visited on his tour of Wales.

The Tea Shop

Once owned by the Marquess of Londonderry, Plas Machynlleth is now the home of Celtica and its recommended tea room. Here you may learn about Welsh and Celtic history through the Celtica audio-visual experience. The tea room was once the drawing room of the mansion. The extensive menu includes soup, baked potatoes, sandwiches and a variety of home-made cakes. Open daily, 10.00am to 6.00pm. Tel: 01654 702702.

The Walk

1. From the car park, walk out to the main road and turn right. In about 40 metres, bear right through gates and follow a track. Pass the Leisure Centre on your right and go left to pass Plas Machynlleth (Celtica).

   Plas Machynlleth dates from the 17th century, but has later additions. It used to be known as Greenfields. In the early 19th century, the mansion was owned by Sir John Edwards, but it passed to the Londonderry family when his only child, Mary, married Henry Vane-Tempest in 1846. Henry became the fifth Marquess of Londonderry. Many famous people have visited the Plas over the years, including King George V and Queen Mary. The mansion and its grounds were given to the town of Machynlleth during the first half of the 20th century.

2. Continue along a path beside a children's playground. Go through gates at West Lodge and, immediately, bear left on a path known as the Roman Steps.

The Dyfi Valley from above the Roman Steps

WALK 20 - MACHYNLLETH

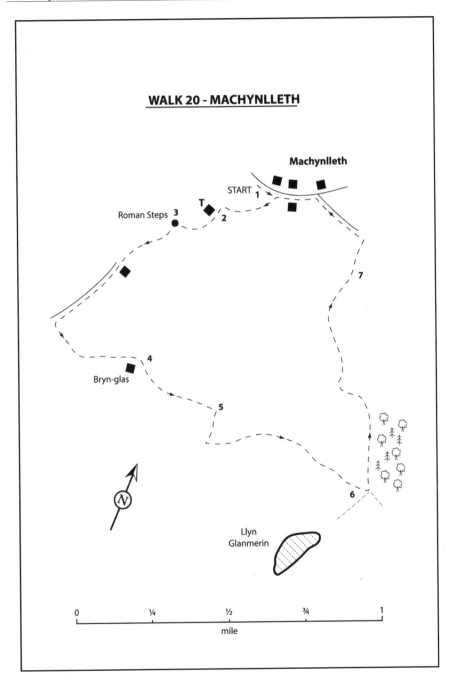

Machynlleth

START 1

Roman Steps 3

T

2

7

4

Bryn-glas

5

6

Llyn
Glanmerin

0   ¼   ½   ¾   1

mile

N

The Roman Steps were probably cut much later than the Roman period but they may have used the pathway to their lookout position on Wylfa, the hill above the steps. The Romans had a fort at Pennal, about four miles west.

3. Climb the steps and follow the path to a kissing gate. Cross a track near houses and continue along a grassy path to the lane. Turn left, uphill. A few metres after the lane starts to go downhill, go through a gate on the left and follow a track. In about 100 metres, it bears to the left and has a stream below on the right. Walk uphill through trees and go through a gate. Veer right and pass Bryn-glas farmhouse on your right.

4. Walk on, uphill, along the track. When it veers right into a field, leave it to continue ahead. Go through a gate and maintain your direction. At a fork, ignore the left-hand track. In about another 50 metres, ignore a track on the right. As you walk uphill, views open up of the Dyfi valley below on your left. After passing a small fenced enclosure (an archaeological dig), the track bends right at some outcrops.

5. Continue on the main track through moorland. In approximately 200 metres, it bears to the left and gradually climbs to a gate. Walk on along the track and, after passing between a few boulders, go slightly downhill to a fence corner. Keep the fence on your right until, after a slight dip, the path veers away from the fence to a path junction. The walk goes left here but, if you would like a view of Llyn Glanmerin, bear right to a stile and walk through an area of felled forest to another stile, and view of the lake.

6. Go back to the path junction and veer left downhill on a clear path to have views of Machynlleth. Ignore other paths leading off and descend to trees and a wall. Follow the wall on your left and walk above a golf course. The path zigzags and eventually passes beside a fence on the left to a stile.

7. Walk ahead to a road and turn left. On reaching a crossroads, bear left into the centre of Machynlleth and the starting place of the walk.

21. Corris

Route: A varied walk taking in lanes, tracks and forest paths. The return is through fields beside the lovely Afon Dulas.

Distance: 5½ miles.

How to get there: Corris Craft Centre is on the A487, north of Machynlleth.

Public Transport: Buses from Dolgellau and Machynlleth.

Start: Car park at the Corris Craft Centre.

Map: Explorer OL23.

Corris is a former slate quarry village surrounded by forest and hills. Braich Goch, the largest quarry near the village, was worked almost continuously from the 1830s to 1971. Slate was transported by horse-drawn tramway to Derwenlas on Afon Dyfi until the opening of the Corris Railway in 1867. After the quarry closed, the slate tips were used as infill and the area landscaped. The Corris Craft Centre

A woodland path near Corris

complex now occupies the site, whilst its access road is the former tramway.

The Tea Shop

Located next to the Tourist Information Centre, the Corris Craft Centre Café is a large, pleasant self-service café with outdoor tables. The menu includes jacket potatoes, rolls, Welsh rarebit, scones and home-made cakes. Hot meals are usually available from 11.30am to 3.00pm. Open 10.00am to 5.00pm daily, April until October.

The Walk

1. From the Craft Centre and car park, return to the access lane and turn right. When the lane bends right to the road, leave it to walk ahead through a gate and follow the old tramway. Just before it ends, go right on a path to the road. Cross with care and turn left along the pavement. At the end of a lay-by on the right, and just before a left bend in the road, bear right on a track downhill. Take a path on the right to cross a footbridge over Afon Deri.

    On the east bank of Afon Deri is Aber Corris Nature Reserve. This three acre patch of ancient broadleaved woodland is predominantly oak, birch and sycamore. Look out for grey wagtail, dipper and pied flycatcher. The reserve is managed by the North Wales Wildlife Trust.

2. Walk up to a lane and turn right. In about half a mile it descends to a crossroads in Corris. Cross directly to another lane and walk downhill to cross a bridge over Afon Dulas. Go uphill and pass a drive on the right to Fron Felen Hall. In another 100 metres, when the lane starts to descend, turn left on a path into forest. Ignore a rough track on the left and continue uphill to meet a broad forest track.

3. Turn left uphill to an area of felled forest. On reaching a fork, go left downhill and follow a track that curves around Nant Gallt-y-Rhiw. Ignore a track on the right and take a narrow, waymarked path on the left. At first, it passes below the forest track, then descends through the forest to a gate. Walk on beside a right-hand fence to join a track and bear right to a gate. Ford a stream and walk on to emerge on another track.

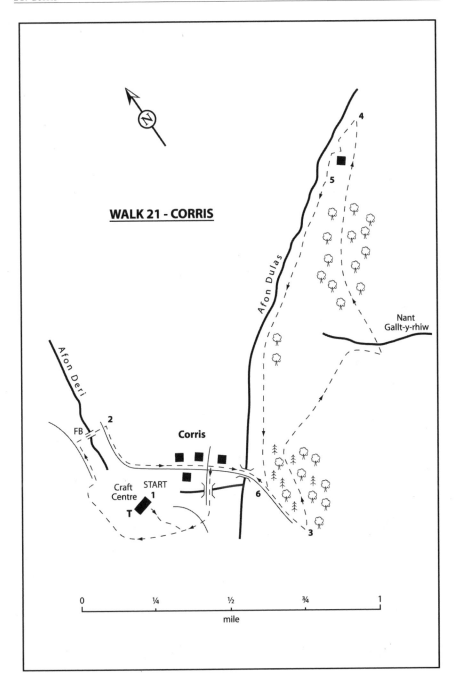

WALK 21 - CORRIS

4. Turn left and go through a gate. Do not cross the bridge ahead, but bear left on a track. It soon bears right in the direction of a house and crosses the stream. In a few metres, veer right in the direction of a telegraph pole. Pass a garden wall on the left and go through a kissing gate into a field. Walk on to have Afon Dulas on your right.

5. Walk through three fields by crossing stiles close to the river, then pass through some trees and ford a stream. Cross the next field further distant from the river and pass a fenced enclosure on the left. Go through a gate into woodland and follow a track uphill to pass above a quarry. Continue on a path beside a fence and emerge on the lane walked earlier.

6. Turn right and cross the bridge over Afon Dulas. At the lane junction, bear left and cross the bridge spanning Afon Deri. In a few metres, when the Railway Museum is on your left, take a path on the right. It goes uphill and bears left to the A487. Cross the road directly to a path and follow the old road for about 100 metres before going right, and left, along the access road to the car park and café.

22. Aberdyfi

Route: A gradual climb on paths to a ridge top lane above Happy Valley. The longer walk continues to the secluded Bearded Lake. There are superb views throughout the walk.

Distance: 4½ or 7½ miles.

How to get there: Aberdyfi is on the A493, south-west of Machynlleth.

Public Transport: Aberdyfi is on the Cambrian Coast Machynlleth-Pwllheli railway line. Buses from Dolgellau and Machynlleth.

Start: Car park on the sea front in Aberdyfi.

Map: Explorer OL23.

Aberdyfi is a charming small seaside resort situated where the River Dyfi flows into Cardigan Bay. The village became famous in 1785 when Charles Dibdin composed the song 'The Bells of Aberdovey', and the lyrics were sung in the Drury Lane musical 'Liberty Hall'.

Aberdyfi: popular watersports centre

The words refer to the submerged church bells of the legendary Cantre'r Gwaelod. According to the story, where Cardigan Bay is now, there was once a fertile plain with sixteen cities that were protected from the sea by a system of dykes and sluices. In the 6th century, during the reign of Gwyddno Garanhir, a drunken guard called Seithennin neglected his duty of maintaining the system. A storm breached the walls and the area was inundated. The towns and their inhabitants were lost for ever. Some people say that on windless summer nights the sound of distant chimes rise from the seabed. According to geologists, an inundation took place in Cardigan Bay at the end of the last Ice Age.

For a few years in the 12th century, there was a castle on the hill above Aberdyfi. Erected by Rhys ap Gruffudd, it was destroyed after a few years by the Normans. Aberdyfi made history again in 1216, when Llywelyn ap Iorwerth held a meeting of Welsh rulers on the banks of the River Dyfi. In 1569, Aberdyfi had only three houses, but the estuary was popular with herring fishermen. Two hundred years later, Aberdyfi had a maritime trade with wheat, barley and corn being the main imports. Timber and oak bark were exported, and, also, stockings made on looms from local wool. By the mid 19th century, there were seven shipyards near the mouth of the River Dyfi at Penhelig. Forty-five sailing ships were built between 1840 and 1880. A road was built along the coast in the early 19th century. Before that, transport between the north and south sides of the estuary was by ferry.

A section of railway was built between Aberdyfi and Llwyngwril in 1863. When the railway was built to the east of Aberdyfi, four years later, the line was taken through two long tunnels behind the village, so as not to spoil the sea front. The excavated rock was used as a foundation for Penhelig terrace and the nearby park, A few years later, a large jetty was built to enable ships to load and unload at all states of the tide. Shipping decreased from about the time of the 1914 to 1918 war and, since then, the harbour area has been rebuilt. Nowadays, Aberdyfi is a popular sailing centre.

The Tea Shop

The cosy Sea Breeze Tea Room is located opposite the beach and car park in Aberdyfi. Home-made cakes, treacle tart, pastries, sandwiches and cream teas are on offer. There are tables outside. The Sea Breeze is also a guest house. Open 10.30am to 5.00pm daily in the summer months. Open weekends only early and late in the season, but it is advisable to check. Tel: 01654 767449.

The Walk

1. From the car park, turn right and pass the Tourist Information Centre on your right. Pass the church on your left and continue along the sea front to the Literary Institute. When the pavement ends, walk on along the road for a few metres, then turn left uphill on a footpath.

2. Follow the path uphill to a lane. Turn right and, almost immediately, go left up steps. On reaching a fork, bear right to a track. Turn right and, in a few paces, go left uphill on a wide track. Follow it around a bend to a footpath. Walk uphill through gorse to a stile then continue ahead, slanting slightly left to a small slate tip.

3. Turn right through a flat area and, in about 50 metres, go slightly left on a clear path to have fine views of the Dyfi estuary to your right. The path soon bears left above a valley. Go through a small gate and walk on to another. In about another 50 metres, climb a stile and go uphill to cross a stream and more stiles on your right. Walk uphill through the field and, before it ends, go left through a gap. Veer right uphill and go through a gap in the bushes into another field. Walk on towards the left side of farm buildings.

4. Go through a gate and emerge on a farm access track. Turn left through another gate and follow the track to a lane. Turn right uphill and, in about 800 metres, cross a cattle grid. For a few hundred metres, the lane is unfenced. When it becomes fenced again, walk on to have fine views of Happy Valley on your left.

   The valley was known as Cwm Dyffryn before the Victorians gave it the name Happy Valley. The Turnpike Trust built a road through it in 1775 to connect Machynlleth with Tywyn. The road leaves the Dyfi valley near Pennal and rises about 500 feet before making a gradual descent through the valley to the A493 south of Tywyn.

5. In 400 metres, just before a field gate on your left, there is a field gate on your right. If you are not walking on as far as the Bearded

Lake, go through the right-hand gate and skip all directions before point 8. If following the longer route, continue along the lane and cross a stile at a gate across it. Follow the lane through another gate and walk on to a house. Go through a gate to pass the house on your left and, immediately, bear right. The track soon bends left uphill and gives fine views of the Dyfi estuary. Cross a ladder stile and, when the wall ends on your right in about 250 metres, look for an inscribed stone on your left.

The stone is inscribed Craig Carn March Arthur. Beside it there is a rock which appears to have the impression of a horse's hoof. According to legend, the mark was left by King Arthur's horse when it jumped across the Dyfi estuary to escape pursuers,

6. Follow the track to a stile at a gate and, in a few metres, take the left-hand (north) fork. In about 300 metres, go over a small rise to the Bearded Lake (Llyn Barfog).

Water lilies grow on the Bearded Lake in the summer and they may have given the lake its name. Alternatively, it may come from the legendary bearded monster said to have been removed from the lake by King Arthur and dragged to Llyn Cau under Cader Idris. The Bearded Lake is traditionally the home of the King of the Fairies, Gwyn ap Nudd. Long ago, fairy ladies sometimes visited the lake with their white dogs and cattle. A local farmer captured one of the cows and she produced a huge amount of milk and many calves. When the cow became old, the greedy farmer decided to fatten her for the butcher. On the day of the slaughter, as the butcher was about to kill the cow, a lady in green appeared on the nearby hill and called the cattle. The farmer and butcher were struck motionless whilst the cow and all her progeny crossed the hill and followed the fairy lady into the lake. Although the farmer and butcher were released from the spell, the cattle were never seen again.

7. Return by your outward route to the point where the short walk leaves the lane by a gate (now on your left and about 200 metres beyond the ladder stile and gate across the lane).

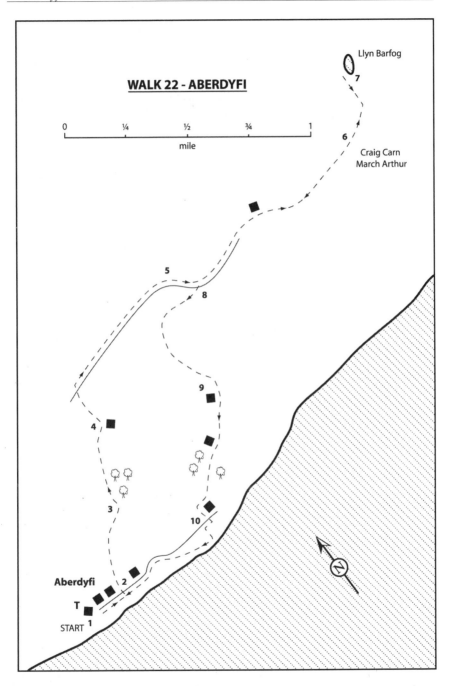

WALK 22 - ABERDYFI

Llyn Barfog

Craig Carn
March Arthur

Aberdyfi

START

mile

8. Bear half-right towards a fence corner. Walk on beside the fence and, when it starts to veer a little to the left, walk ahead downhill and go through a field gate. Veer slightly left and cross a track. In a few more metres, cross a stile at a gate and go downhill. Walk above trees on your left and follow the path steeply downhill. Keep above the stream and walk on to a stile.

9. Follow the path to a farm and bear right between buildings. Pass the farmhouse and veer left over a cattle grid. After crossing another cattle grid, climb a ladder stile on the right. The path goes uphill and soon bears left through woodlands. Go through a gate and follow a path above a left-hand fence. When the fence descends steeply, stay on the high path along the edge of the woods. At the end of the trees, go right uphill to grassland and then downhill to a track. Cross and veer slightly right towards the left side of pines. Go through a gap in the trees and bear left. At an access track, bear right and, in a few paces, go left downhill. Take a footpath on your right and follow the left-hand fence. After crossing a stile and stream, walk down to a stile and the A493.

10. Turn right and, at a small parking area in about 100 metres, go left on a footbridge over the railway line to the promontory called Picnic Island. Bear right downhill and beside the railway to some steps. Pass below a wall then go up steps and follow the rock path to gardens at Penhelig. Emerge on the road and turn left to follow it into Aberdyfi.

23. Tywyn

Route: An easy, level walk to an attractive lake and the River Dysynni. The return passes St Cadfan's Church.

Distance: 5 miles.

How to get there: Tywyn is on the A493, north-west of Machynlleth.

Public Transport: Tywyn is on the Cambrian Coast Line. Buses run from Machynlleth and Dolgellau.

Start: Car park on the sea front in Tywyn.

Map: Explorer OL23.

Originally a village located near marshland and set back some distance from the sea, Tywyn has gradually expanded into a spacious seaside resort. A long street links the sea front with the town Centre. Beyond the southern end of the promenade a three mile beach stretches south to Aberdyfi, whilst from the northern outskirts of the town are wide views of the surrounding hills and the Dysynni valley.

One of the recommended tea rooms in Tywyn

The Tea Shops

There are two possible places for refreshments.

Located at the beginning and end of the walk, and opposite the promenade, the Town and Gown Tea Room is in a 200-year-old building, which was once a farmhouse. Baguettes, salads, soup, cream teas and a fine selection of cakes are on offer. There are tables outside, and meals are served on some evenings in an upstairs restaurant. You may like to browse amongst the second-hand books that are for sale. Open 10.00am to 6.00pm in the summer, 11.00am to 4.00pm at the beginning and end of the season. Tel: 01654 711771.

On the way back to the start, the walk passes The Proper Gander Restaurant and Tea Room in the High Street. The varied menu includes hot snacks, jacket potatoes and sandwiches plus a choice of afternoon teas. Take your pick from Gosling, Goose or greedy Gander (fruit scone, bara brith plus sponge cake and cream). Open 10.00am to 4.30pm on Mondays to Saturdays (10.30am to 4.00pm in the winter). Open 10.30am to 3.00pm on Sundays (10.30am to 2.00pm in the winter). Also open on some evenings. Tel: 01654 711270.

The Walk

1. On the sea front, walk along the promenade with the beach on your left. At the end of the parking area, go down steps to continue along the sea front. On nearing a static caravan park, go right on a surfaced track and continue on a road. Go over a level crossing and, immediately, turn left along a road. Pass a children's playground and, at the end of the houses, go right on a track.

2. Go through a gate and, in a few paces, bear left on the track. On reaching a tall pole, go left a few paces, then right to cross a stile and footbridge over a channel. Slant right in the direction of Broad Water. The path may be vague at first, but it soon becomes clearer and passes through some gorse before joining another path at the lakeside. Turn right to have Broad Water on your left.

   Broad Water is a popular place for bird watching. Heron, shelduck, mallard, merganser and waders may be seen. Keep a

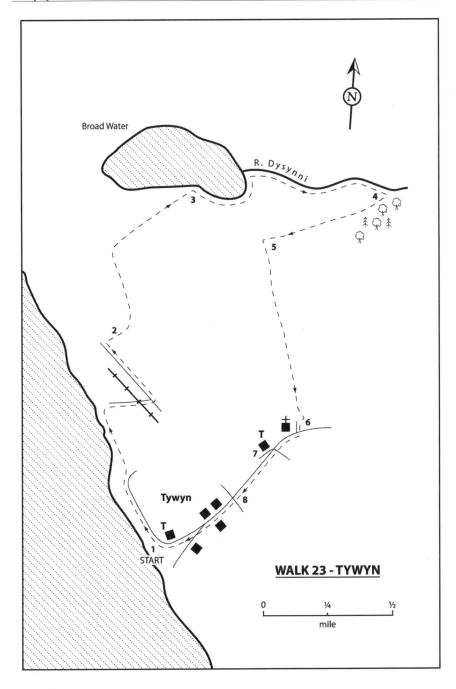

Broad Water

R. Dysynni

N

3

4

5

2

6

T

7

8

Tywyn

T

1

START

WALK 23 - TYWYN

0   ¼   ½

mile

watch for cormorants flying up the Dysynni valley to Bird Rock.

3.   Walk along an embankment and cross a stile. The embankment bears right at the point where Broad Water meets the River Dysynni. When the embankment nears a wood, bear right to have a channel and the trees on your left.

4.   Follow the channel through fields. In about 900 metres, go through a gate into a narrow field and walk ahead to join a track near sheep pens. Turn left through the sheep pens and a gate.

5.   Ignore a footbridge on the right and go ahead along a track. Pass through a gate across the track and walk on between channels. The track becomes surfaced and passes houses before emerging on the A493 near St Cadfan's Church in Tywyn.

St Cadfan came from Brittany in the 6th century and settled near a well not far from the site of the present church in Tywyn. With others, he established a small community centred around prayer and the growing of food. He founded a monastery on Bardsey Island. Vikings burnt two of the early wooden churches in Tywyn and the present church dates from the 12th century. Inside is the Cadfan Stone which bears ancient inscriptions in Welsh. Dated from the 5th to the 7th centuries, they are probably the oldest written examples of the Welsh language. There are also two 14th-century effigies.

6.   Bear right and, in about 100 metres, you will pass a small roundabout. A little further on, when a road with a small memorial is on your left, The Proper Gander Restaurant and Tea Room is on your right.

7.   To return to the sea front, take the road on the left. Pass council buildings and the library on your right. Go over a crossroads to the Talyllyn Railway Wharf Station.

The Talyllyn narrow gauge railway was originally opened in the 1860s to carry slate from quarries near Abergynolwyn to the main line railway at Tywyn. Passenger services followed a year or two later. After the quarries closed in the mid 20th century, railway enthusiasts formed a preservation society, the first of its kind. Trains now run from Tywyn to its terminus, high above Abergynolwyn, at Nant Gwernol.

8. Walk on along Neptune Road and cross a bridge over the main line railway. Follow the road around a right bend to the beach and sea front. Turn right and, in a few metres, Town and Gown Tea Room is on your right.

24. Llwyngwril

Route: This long walk along moorland tracks, paths and lanes is rewarded with magnificent views of the coastline and Mawddach estuary. Try to choose a clear day.

Distance: 9½ miles.

How to get there: Llwyngwril is on the A493 between Tywyn and Dolgellau.

Public Transport: Llwyngwril is on the Machynlleth – Pwllheli Cambrian Coast Railway Line. Buses from Dolgellau and Machynlleth.

Start: Car park in Ffordd yr Orsaf off the A493 near the bridge in Llwyngwril.

Map: Explorer OL23.

Llwyngwril is a pleasant village on the coast road between Tywyn and Fairbourne. The little River Gwril passes under a bridge in the centre of the village on its journey from the mountains to the sea. An ancient track, with a succession of Bronze Age standing stones, climbs the hillside from Llwyngwril to high above the Mawddach estuary. Some stones are very close together and the reason for their alignment remains a mystery.

The Tea Shop

Oriel Llwyngwril Gallery and Tea Room is located in the old church rooms alongside the A493. Gifts of a wide variety are on sale, including paintings, pottery and beeswax candles. The tea room serves light lunches, snacks, fruit tarts and a good selection of cakes. There are tables outside. Open 10.00am to 7.00pm from May to October and 10.00am to 4.30pm from November to April. Open seven days a week. Tel: 01341 250054.

The Walk

1. From the car park in Ffordd yr Orsaf, go right to the A493 and turn left over the bridge. In a few metres, turn right on a dead end lane. Bear left with the lane and ignore a track on the right. After passing houses, go through a gate across the lane and walk on,

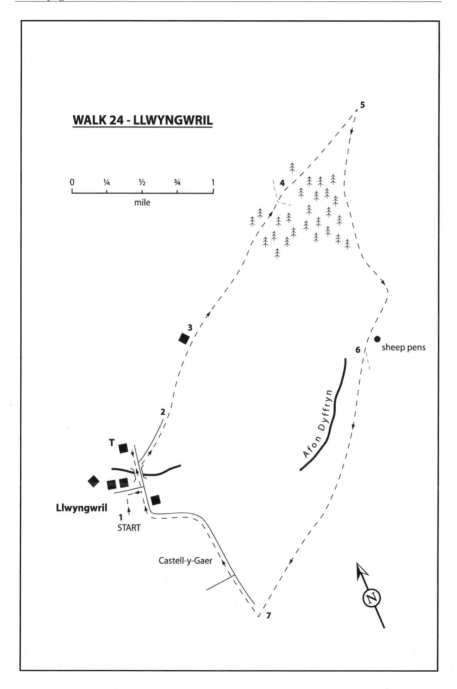

WALK 24 - LLWYNGWRIL

0   ¼   ½   ¾   1

mile

5

4

3

2

T

Llwyngwril

1
START

Castell-y-Gaer

sheep pens

6

Afon Dyffryn

7

N

uphill. When the surfaced lane bends right to a gate, continue ahead on a grassy track between walls.

2. When the walls end, the track continues between fences with views to the sea. Go through a gate and walk on across the gorse-covered hillside and, further on, open land. Pass above a ruin and continue through gates. Pass a farm and ponds below on the left and join a surfaced track.

3. Turn right and, after passing through three gates across the lane, look for standing stones in a field on your left. Further on are splendid open views of the coast and Mawddach estuary. The lane goes downhill to a gate and enters forest. Walk on to reach a point where there are fields on the left. At a footpath signpost, ignore the first steep path on the right, but take the second path.

4. The path rises gradually up the hill and emerges from the forest. Cross a stile and continue through open moorland. After crossing another stile, walk on beside a left-hand wall. Pass a memorial plaque and join the track above.

5. Turn right and go through gates across the track, then pass above the forest. Ignore paths leading off and walk on through moor-

The ancient track from Llwyngwril

land. Just over half a mile from the forest, the track bears right to a cattle grid. In another 600 metres, look for sheep pens in a field on your left. In about another 100 metres, at a left bend in the track, leave it for a rutted grassier track on the right.

6. This track runs below the firmer track and, in about 500 metres, passes small slate tips. Below, to your right, is the River Dyffryn. Walk on through moorland and pass through a gate to have a wall on your right. At a fork, in another 400 metres, keep right, beside a wall. Go through a gate across the track and walk on, alongside a fence. Pass some coniferous trees and, when the fence ends at a junction of tracks, continue ahead. Pass under the wires of pylons and maintain your direction to meet a fence on the left. Continue ahead and, a few metres before reaching a gate, cross a ladder stile on the right.

7. Follow the right-hand boundary of the field to a tall ladder stile, then cross the next field to another stile. Emerge on a lane and turn right to a fork. Take the right-hand lane and walk downhill. After crossing a cattle grid, you will see the mound of Castell y Gaer on your left.

> Castell y Gaer is a small Iron Age hill fort overlooking the sea. The flat top of the hill was once surrounded by a stone rampart thought to be four metres thick with an entrance on the south-east side. On the south side, there were two ditches.

8. The lane descends steeply to emerge on the A493. Turn right and take Ffordd yr Orsaf to return to the start or, to visit the tea room, cross the bridge and walk on for about another 100 metres. Llwyngwril Gallery is on your left.

25. Dolgellau

Route: A level walk along an old railway trackbed is followed by an easy climb through woodlands to quiet lanes with superb views of the surrounding mountains.

Distance: 6 miles.

How to get there: Dolgellau lies north of Machynlleth, near the junction of the A494 and A470.

Public Transport: Buses from Aberystwyth, Wrexham, Barmouth and other nearby towns.

Start: Car park near the bridge across Afon Wnion.

Map: Explorer OL23.

Backed by the mountain range of Cader Idris, the small town of Dolgellau stands at the confluence of the Rivers Aran and Wnion. Lying in the centre of a sheep farming area, the town grew around the woollen industry and, in the 18th century, almost every household owned a hand loom. The cloth was finished at small fulling mills before being sent down the river to Barmouth for export, some to America.

Dolgellau has many historic buildings. The bridge spanning the River Wnion dates from 1638 whilst the buildings in Eldon Square are 200 years old. Built in the 18th century, St Mary's Church has timber columns brought over the mountain pass from Dinas Mawddwy and an effigy of Meurig ap Ynyr Fychan who died about 1350. Owain Glyndwr held a Welsh Parliament in the town in the early 1400s.

After George Fox visited Dolgellau in 1657, many local people became Quakers. Because they would not swear any kind of oath, they were persecuted and some were imprisoned. William Penn acquired land for the Quakers in America, and this became Pennsylvania. Many Welsh Quakers emigrated and one of them was Rowland Ellis who lived at Bryn Mawr in the Cader Idris foothills. He called his new home Bryn Mawr and, later on, this name was given to an American women's college.

The Tea Shop

Yr Hen Efail is conveniently close to the car park and end of the walk. The varied menu includes main meals, jacket potatoes, sandwiches and a selection of delicious home-made cakes and tarts. There are outdoor tables. Open 10.00am to 5.00pm, Monday to Saturday. Also open on Bank Holiday Sundays and on Sundays during school summer holidays. Open mid March to mid October. Tel: 01341 422977.

The Walk

1. Leave the car park by having the river close by on your right, and take a path – signed 'Mawddach Trail' – beside the recreation ground. In about 500 metres, cross a footbridge spanning the river and, in a few paces, go left along a track. The river is now on your left. At the end of the track, emerge on a road. Cross carefully and bear right a few metres, then go left to follow another section of the Mawddach Trail.

The Mawddach Trail

The Mawddach Trail is a cycleway and footpath linking Dolgellau and Barmouth. It follows the trackbed of the Ruabon to Barmouth railway line to Morfa Mawddach. The line opened in the 1860s, but closed almost exactly one hundred years later in 1965. The trackbed passes the Penmaenpool reedbed, where otters and wetland birds such as redshank breed.

2. Pass a parking area and cross a bridge. Continue along the tree lined track, passing reed-beds. Emerge in a car park near the old signal box at Penmaenpool.

The old signal box is now a RSPB bird observatory. It is open at Easter and then weekends until the summer months, when it is open daily until early September. Hours are 11.00am or noon until 4.00pm or 5.00pm. Many estuary birds can be spotted from the site.

The toll bridge dates from 1879 and could be opened for ships. The nearby George III hotel, originally an inn and ship chandler's premises, dates from 1650. Gerard Manley Hopkins stayed here and is reputed to have written the poem "Penmaenpool" in a guest book. Along the inlets of the River Mawddach were many boatyards where sloops were built of oak from the surrounding woodlands.

3. From the car park, go up to a road, and turn right. In about 200 metres, go left at a footpath signpost. Pass below a house and follow the path as it curves right to a small gate. Emerge on an access lane and turn left through woodlands. In about 600 metres, at a pool on the left screened by trees, go right uphill on a waymarked, narrow path.

4. Cross a ladder stile and walk ahead through trees, to a track. Turn right along it and ignore a right-hand fork. Go through a gate to pass a cottage on the right, then bear left through the garden to a small gate. Walk straight ahead down the field to pass a small wooded hummock on the right. Pass trees on the right and go through a broken wall to a gate. Walk uphill with a fence on the left and cross a ladder stile on the right. Go left on a path above a house to a stile and field. Cross to another stile and turn left on the lane.

5. Go through a gate and bear right along this scenic, undulating lane. On your right are views of the Cader Idris range. The lane passes between fields, through open land and woodlands before bearing right to emerge on a wider lane. Turn left and, after passing the drive to Clogwyn on your right and the Carmelite monastery on your left, turn right along a dead end lane.

6. The lane rises and soon levels before rising again to pass some terraced houses. Ignore a footpath on the left and follow the lane around a bend. After passing the last house, go left on a track. In about 40 metres, leave it to take a path on the right. Emerge on a road and go left towards Dolgellau town centre. Bear right along Meyrick Street, then left through Eldon Square to the car park and tea room.

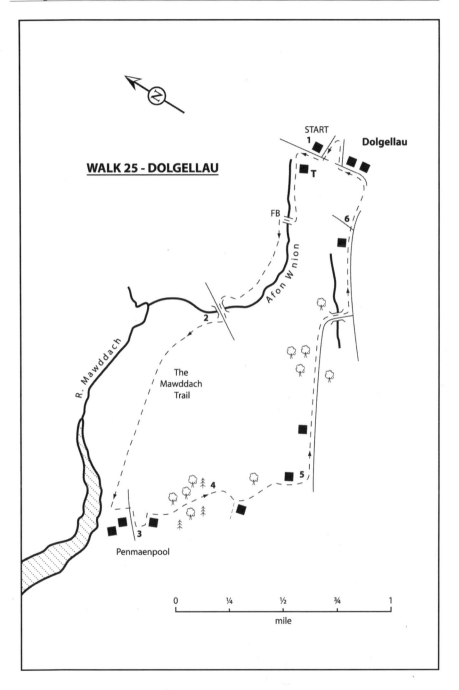

WALK 25 - DOLGELLAU

START
Dolgellau

FB

Afon Wnion

R. Mawddach

The
Mawddach
Trail

Penmaenpool

| 0 | ¼ | ½ | ¾ | 1 |
mile